Harriet Crawford presents a scholarly and up-to-date account of the archaeology of the Arabian Gulf from *c*. 4500–1500 BC. It offers a new interpretation of the structure of society in the Early Dilmun period (*c*. 2000–1700 BC)
using material from the recently excavated site of Saar on the main Bahrain
island. The urban, centralized and probably literate society in Dilmun is contrasted with the contemporary societies in Oman and the Emirates. Here there
is evidence from buildings and graves for a loosely knit, apparently tribal
society. Both societies were greatly influenced by their participation in the
complex trade routes which linked them with ancient Mesopotamia to the
north and the Indus Valley to the south east, but developed their own distinctive cultures. The reason for their divergent development seems to relate
to the fact that Dilmun was an entrepot, while the Oman peninsula was a
source of raw materials.

DILMUN AND ITS GULF NEIGHBOURS

DILMUN
AND ITS
GULF
NEIGHBOURS

HARRIET CRAWFORD

CAMBRIDGE
UNIVERSITY PRESS

PUBLISHED BY THE PRESS SYNDICATE OF THE UNIVERSITY OF CAMBRIDGE
The Pitt Building, Trumpington Street, Cambridge CB2 1RP, United Kingdom

CAMBRIDGE UNIVERSITY PRESS
The Edinburgh Building, Cambridge CB2 2RU, United Kingdom
40 West 20th Street, New York, NY 10011–4211, USA
10 Stamford Road, Oakleigh, Melbourne 3166, Australia

First published 1998

Printed in the United Kingdom at the University Press, Cambridge

Typeset in Apollo 11½/13½   [SF]

A catalogue record for this book is available from the British Library

Library of Congress cataloguing in publication data

Crawford, Harriet E.W.
Dilmun and its Gulf neighbours / Harriet Crawford.
p.   cm.
Includes bibliographical references and index.
ISBN 0 521 58348 9 (hbck) – ISBN 0 521 58679 8 (pbk)
1. Bahrain – Antiquities.   2. Persian Gulf Region – Antiquities.
3. Bahrain – Civilization.   4. Persian Gulf Region – Civilization.
I. Title.
DS247.B23C729   1988
953.65–dc21   97-9527 CIP

ISBN 0 521 58348 9 hardback
ISBN 0 521 58679 8 paperback

CONTENTS

ILLUSTRATIONS

PREFACE AND ACKNOWLEDGEMENTS

In 1989 Robert Killick and Jane Moon invited me to join them in setting up the London–Bahrain Archaeological Expedition (LBAE) to study the economy and society of ancient Dilmun. Thanks to the Ministry of Information of the State of Bahrain we were granted a permit to continue work at the partially excavated site of Saar in the north-west of the island and so began the first extensive investigation of the social and economic structure of Dilmun. I am deeply grateful to my colleagues for offering me the opportunity to take part in this exciting and important undertaking which broke new ground for us all. It also led to my growing interest in the archaeology and social development of the adjacent regions of the Arabian Peninsula. This book is an attempt to synthesize a great deal of rather fragmentary material into some kind of coherent picture of the very different ways in which the two areas developed between the late fourth and the early second millennia. It will inevitably be somewhat out of date by the time it appears as new material is becoming available almost every month. This is the result of an upsurge in archaeological work over the last ten years which is intensifying rather than declining. In spite of this, I hope that students will find that this book fills a gap in the admirable framework provided by works such as Professor D.T. Potts' *The Arabian Gulf in Prehistory* which concentrate largely on the basic data, rather than its interpretation.

Many people have helped me in the preparation of this book and my deepest debt is to Professor Marlies Heinz and Michael Rice who found time to plough through early drafts of the manuscript. The finished product benefitted enormously from their kind, constructive, and knowledgeable criticism. It is a great pleasure to acknowledge my debt to them both. I have also been fortunate in being able to discuss many points with my colleague at the Institute of Archaeology, Carl Phillips, who has been most generous with his time and information.

The drawings and photographs come from many sources and once again I must thank Robert Killick and Jane Moon for allowing me to use so much of the Saar material. The interpretations are my own, and do not necessarily reflect their views. The drawings are the work of Ruth Carter, Tessa Rickards and Duncan Woodburn all of whom have shown themselves endlessly patient and skilful. In addition the following have kindly given me permission to use drawings or photographs of which they hold the copyright: The National Museum of Bahrain, Shirley Kay, Derek Kennett, Carl Phillips, Michael Rice and Michael Roaf.

Finally, my husband Peter, who despairs of my punctuation, dealt with my commas with a kindly, but firm hand. Thank you all.

ABBREVIATIONS

AAE.	Arabian Archaeology and Epigraphy.
ARET.	Archivi Reali di Ebla, Testi, Rome.
AUAE.	Archaeology in the United Arab Emirates.
BASOR.	Bulletin of the American Schools of Oriental Research.
BBVO.	Berliner Beiträge zum Vorderen Orient.
BTAA.	Bahrain through the ages: the archaeology. eds. Al Khalifa, Shaikha Haya Ali and Michael Rice, Kegan Paul International 1986.
CNI.	Carsten Niebuhr Institute Copenhagen.
DAFI.	Délegation archéologique française en Iran.
JAOS.	Journal of the American Oriental Society.
JASP.	Jutland Archaeological Society Publications.
JOS.	Journal of Oman Studies.
LBAE.	London–Bahrain Archaeological Expedition.
Mus.Cat.	*Bahrain National Museum. Archaeological Collections. PreIslamic antiquities from excavations 1954–1975 I.* eds. Pierre Lombard and Monik Kevran.
PSAS.	Proceedings of the Seminar for Arabian Studies.

GLOSSARY

BARASTI – Light structure built of palm leaves or other organic materials.

FARUSH – Carbonate beach rock formed in shallow lagoons.

QANĀT – Underground water channels linked to a spring and maintained by means of vertical shafts at regular intervals. Together they form an irrigation system which minimises evaporation.

Isin

I R A Q

Uruk

Ubaid

Eridu   Ur

Larsa

Basra

I R A N

KUWAIT

Failaka

A R A B I A N

Abu Khamis

Dosariyah

Ras Tannura
Tarut I.

Dammam
Dhahran

G U L

S A U D I

Abqaiq

Ain Qannas   Uqair

Khor

Ras Abaruk
al Da'asa
QATAR

A R A B I A

Hofuf Oasis

Da

Riyadh ■

Jabrin Oasis

0 _____ 300 km
0 _____ 200 miles

- - - - Routes

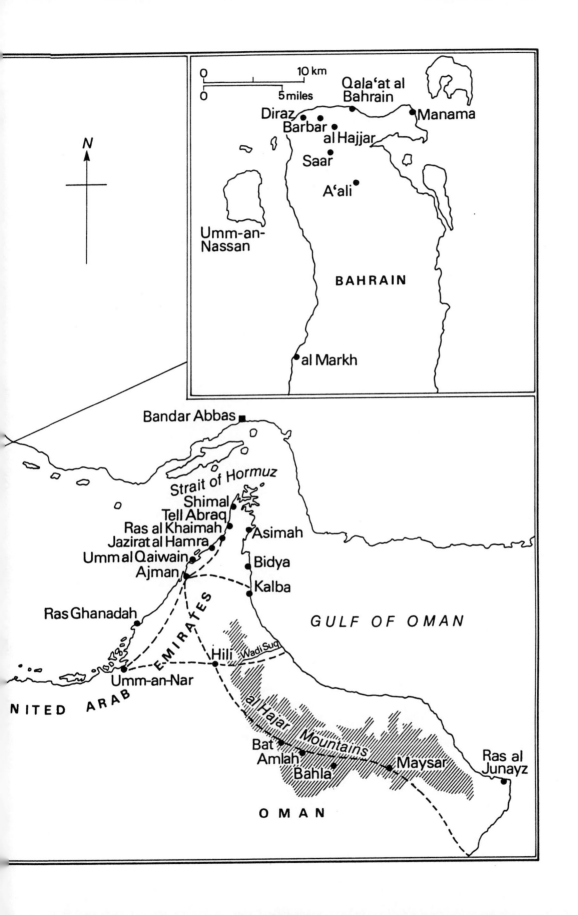

10 km

5 miles

Qala'at al Bahrain

Manama

Diraz

Barbar

al Hajjar

Saar

A'ali

Umm-an-Nassan

BAHRAIN

al Markh

N

Bandar Abbas

Strait of Hormuz

Shimal

Tell Abraq

Ras al Khaimah

Asimah

Jazirat al Hamra

Umm al Qaiwain

Bidya

Ajman

Kalba

GULF OF OMAN

Ras Ghanadah

EMIRATES

Hili

Wadi Suq

Umm-an-Nar

NITED ARAB

al Hajar Mountains

Bat

Amlah

Maysar

Bahla

Ras al Junayz

OMAN

Chapter 1

THE SETTING

The name Dilmun appears on some of the earliest written documents in the world (Fig. 1.1). These are clay tablets inscribed with a rather experimental version of cuneiform which was to become the dominant script of the ancient Near East from about 3000 BC. The tablets were written in the Sumerian language and were found in a temple precinct dedicated to the goddess Inanna in the great southern Mesopotamian city of Uruk. They are dated to the end of the fourth millennium BC. The contents of the documents are strictly practical in nature; they contain lists of goods, of places, and of officials associated with the temple. The adjective Dilmun is used to describe a type of axe and one specific official; in addition there are lists of rations of wool issued to people connected with Dilmun (Englund 1983: 39). We know that the word refers to a geographical location as it is written with letters ki after it, which are only used when writing place names. Although the early texts provide a number of clues about where Dilmun actually was, it is only recently that it has been possible to be reasonably certain of its location, through the piecing together of clues from many different sources. These sources include archaeological evidence and economic, historical and literary documents. Some of these describe the location directly, some its produce and some tell of the stories associated with it.

The early economic texts give us reliable but limited information. They tell us that, from the start, Dilmun was associated with copper, a commodity which is found only in a limited number of geological conditions. This association provided the first, although as it turned out, rather misleading clue to the location (Englund 1983). Timber, dates and 'fish eyes', possibly the ancient name for pearls, are also mentioned repeatedly in the third and second millennium sources. All these goods, as well as other, more exotic ones, were brought by boat from Dilmun to Mesopotamia.

The later economic and historical texts also provide us with further quasi-geographical clues. The land of Dilmun is variously said to have lain 'in the middle of the

1.1 'Dilmun' in the cuneiform script. The determinative 'ki' is not shown.

1

sea', 'in the land of the rising sun', and 'at the mouth of the great rivers'. (For a complete list of references in the Mesopotamian texts see Heimpel 1987.) Other texts associate it with two other countries, Magan and Meluhha, placing it nearer to Mesopotamia than to either of them. Magan is usually identified as the Oman Peninsula and Meluhha as the Indus valley (Gelb 1970). For example, Sargon of Agade, *c.* 2350 BC, claims in a famous inscription that ships from Dilmun, Magan and Meluhha moored at his capital city of Akkad. Much later, Sargon II of Assyria describes Dilmun as lying thirty *beru* from Sumer, in the middle of the sea (Cornwall 1946; Alster 1983: 45–6). This confirms the information gathered from the earlier documents suggesting that some or all of the territory of Dilmun was an island. As a *beru* is usually thought to have been a measure of time equivalent to two hours, it also provides us with an approximate travelling time from Mesopotamia. If we assume that a boat could travel about ten miles per *beru* or two-hour period, we deduce that this island lay about 300 miles from the shores of southern Mesopotamia. As the evidence from the Agade inscription and other similar examples suggests that Dilmun was closer than either Magan or Meluhha, modern Oman and the Indus valley respectively, this distance of 300 miles would fit well.

The literary texts also tell us that the island was notable for its sweet water springs. Bahrain is the largest island in the Arabian Gulf north of Oman, it is roughly 300 miles south of the mouth of the Shatt al Arab and is famous for the artesian springs of fresh water which well up on land and even in the sea. In addition, until recently Bahrain was renowned for both dates and pearls. It also served as an entrepot for the copper mined in Oman so, although no copper occurs naturally on the island, the association with copper in the texts from the Uruk III period onwards can be explained by Bahrain's function as a market. On the basis of all these factors it must be the prime candidate for identification as Dilmun.

The convincing but circumstantial evidence for the identification of Dilmun with Bahrain is further strengthened by one of the few cuneiform inscriptions found on Bahrain itself. It was engraved on a large black stone shaped like a shoe, presumably part of a statue, found preserved in a mosque, and first reported by Captain Durand in 1878. Sadly, it has since disappeared and is thought to have been destroyed in the London blitz. The foot was dedicated to the god Inzak of Agarum by a man called Rimum. This god is referred to in the cuneiform sources as the chief god of Dilmun and the son of the Mesopotamian water god Enki (Alster 1983; al Nashef 1986).

The second millennium literary texts from Mesopotamia add another more romantic dimension to the picture of Dilmun. They describe it as a pure and holy place, a paradise of sweet running water and lush vegetation where the great god Enki impregnated the goddess Ninhursag in one of the Sumerian creation myths (Alster 1983: 54–9). Gilgamesh, the Sumerian hero, also travelled to Dilmun across the sea in his quest for eternal life and it was there that he met with Ziusudra, the survivor of the great flood, who was granted immortality by the gods for his role in perpetuating the human race.

There is a curious dichotomy in the picture of Dilmun presented by the literary and economic texts. On one hand, as we have seen, it was known as an important market-place trading in copper and a variety of other staples and luxury goods. On the other it was seen as the pure land of streams and gardens, inhabited by gods and demi-gods. The earliest written reference we have to the Paradise Dilmun dates to the early second millennium and so is much later than the references to it as a source of copper and wood. The myths themselves are probably much older than this because it is generally accepted that such stories had a long oral history before they were finally codified and written down (Finley 1954). We can guess, then, that the mythical picture of Dilmun may have evolved in the early third millennium. Significantly, this is a period when there seems to have been little direct contact between Dilmun and southern Mesopotamia.

This lack of actual contact would make it easier to explain how such an idealized picture might have evolved. It is hard to see how hard-nosed merchants and sailors would have painted such an unreal picture if they had been in regular commercial contact with the islands. On the other hand, it is possible to imagine that rumours of Bahrain's springs and vegetation might have been picked up by the traders travelling south down the coast of Arabia from the fifth millennium onwards and that by the time direct commercial contacts were established with the islands, towards the middle of the third millennium, the paradise image was already deeply entrenched in mythology. A somewhat similar situation can perhaps be seen in nineteenth-century Western Europe where Jerusalem, which in much of the medieval period was inaccessible to the West, was seen as a synonym for perfection. By the late nineteenth century enough travellers had visited the city to know that the reality was very different, but its mythical status was too well established to be dented and remained a powerful metaphor. A similar situation may explain the references to an idyllic Dilmun in the early second millennium.

The number of textual references to Dilmun in the Mesopotamian sources, in successive periods of its history, acts as a rough and ready guide to the importance of the region as a trading partner. (The small numbers of tablets involved *in toto* also illustrates the limited and probably unrepresentative nature of the written evidence.) References in the Uruk III texts, *c*.3200 BC, are very few relative to the total number of tablets which exist from this time. This probably reflects the fact that Anatolia was Mesopotamia's major source of metals at this time and that Dilmun copper was not of major economic significance. Raw materials of all sorts seem to have travelled down the Euphrates through the network of so-called Uruk colonies situated in northern Syria and southern Anatolia and this, rather than the sea route up the Gulf, was the primary supply route (Algaze 1993). The number of references to Dilmun then increases very slowly from the second quarter of the third millennium and the name also begins to occur on other types of text, such as royal building inscriptions. By the middle of the millennium, it is also found on tablets from the Syrian city of Ebla (Pettinato 1983). In the Agade period we find the first references to Magan and Meluhha, while Dilmun occurs infrequently. In the Ur III period Dilmun is totally eclipsed by references to Magan for a period of about one hundred years. By the early second millennium the situation is reversed and there is a relatively large number of both commercial and literary references to Dilmun, while Magan disappears. This is the period when trade between Dilmun and the southern Mesopotamian kingdoms of Isin and Larsa was at its height. Slightly later in the early second millennium there are one or two references to Dilmun in archives from Mari, on the middle Euphrates, and Assyria in the north, although few are found in southern Mesopotamia itself.

It is a useful exercise to compare the picture presented by the textual evidence with that derived from the archaeology of the Arabian Gulf. The fairly straightforward picture of gradually intensifying contacts between Mesopotamia and Dilmun from the late fourth millennium onwards, briefly interrupted by closer ties between Mesopotamia and Magan in the Ur III period, is not matched by the material remains. In the first place, finds of fifth- and early fourth millennium Ubaid pottery from Mesopotamia on the main Bahrain island show that relations between the two regions predate the first written evidence. A little later, when we have already seen that there is unambiguous evidence from the economic texts of the later fourth millennium for contact between southern Mesopotamia and Dilmun, the islands of Bahrain seem to have been virtually uninhabited. This period in Mesopotamia is represented by the Uruk and Jemdat Nasr periods, but pottery of this type is virtually absent from Bahrain (Larsen 1983b: 77) and the evidence for any contact with Mesopotamia is very thin. When the indigenous pottery sequence is better defined some local wares may be found to plug the gap, but even if this were to happen it would seem that Bahrain was only inhabited by small groups of fishermen or farmers during this early period. It can hardly have been the centre of a trading network.

The islands only seem to have been extensively inhabited in the second half of the third millennium, despite the fact that the texts suggest steadily increasing contacts from about 2600 BC. The final anomaly is provided by the fact that, in the late third millennium, when the tablets only refer to trade with Magan, Bahrain appears to be more prosperous and in closer contact with Mesopotamia than Oman (Magan) was.

A number of possible solutions have been proposed to explain away some of these discrepancies. It seems possible that the name Dilmun, when it first appears in the late fourth millennium, was a generalized term meaning something as vague as 'Lands far away to the south'. Some support for a more generalized definition of Dilmun comes from a text from Ebla, dating to the middle of the third millennium, in which Subir, a poorly defined area to the north of Sumer, is contrasted with Dilmun, perhaps an equally ill-defined area to the south (*ARET* 5: 7 11.4–12.2). It would be reasonable to suggest that it was only in the later third millennium, when commercial contacts became more regular and more important, that sailors knew the seas well enough to be able to subdivide the great area to the south, known as the Lower Sea, into different geographical parts, each of which then received its own name. This is certainly the time when Magan and Meluhha were recognized as separate entities and their names first appear on the tablets.

A less radical proposal would be that the name Dilmun referred to a rather more specific area than that suggested above, but to something more extensive than just the Bahrain islands. This is an attractive idea, especially as the east coast of Arabia, immediately adjacent to Bahrain, shows some evidence of contacts with Mesopotamia in the late fourth and early third millennia just at the times when Bahrain itself was only sparsely inhabited. The two areas are, of course, very close to each other both geographically and culturally. By the late third millennium the material cultures of the two were almost identical. If the evidence from the Eastern Province and Bahrain is taken together as representative of a single culture, the archaeological and the textual evidence can be made to agree much better.

The idea that the name Dilmun referred to what is now the Eastern Province, as well as to Bahrain itself, is not new. The suggestion was first made by Burrows and Deimal in 1928 and has been discussed regularly since then (e.g. Cornwall 1946; Alster 1983). In addition, both archaeological and textual evidence suggest that in the first third of the second millennium, when Dilmun was at its most important, the name had even wider implications and included the then newly settled island of Failaka off the coast of Kuwait (Fig. 1.2). Here too, the material culture is identical with that on Bahrain and the Eastern Province (chapter 6). There is some slight evidence to suggest that the name may even, sometimes, have embraced part of the Iranian coast as well, although very little is known of the archaeology of this area. Objects and pottery from early explorations at Bushire are identical to pieces from Bahrain, but this may reflect no more than trading links (Howard-Carter 1972). Further support for the suggestion that the same geographical name might have been used for both the islands and parts of the mainland comes, by analogy, from the early Islamic period when the name Bahrain also covered large areas of the mainland (Rice 1984).

A third possibility is that the name Dilmun may have been applied to different locations at different times. This is undoubtedly true of the name Meluhha which in the third millennium was given to the Indus valley, but from the middle of the second millennium probably described Egypt, Nubia or Ethiopia (Alster 1983: 41). There is no evidence to support this suggestion in the case of Dilmun, but it should not be forgotten.

The above paragraphs present an interesting case study which demonstrates the importance of bringing together evidence from both written and archaeological

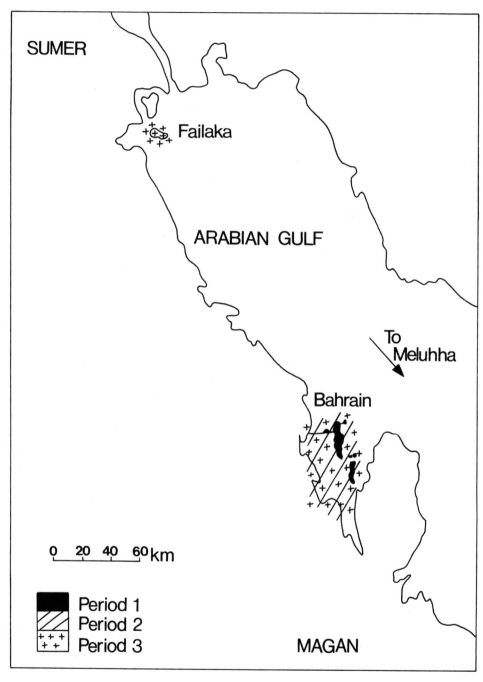

1.2 Map showing extent of Dilmun in the Early Dilmun period and the location of Magan.

sources if an accurate picture is to emerge. Each category of evidence would have given us an internally consistent picture which, when placed in a wider context, is shown to be misleading. In summary, it seems most likely that the name Dilmun described an area whose size varied at different times in its history and which became better defined as time went on. Contact with Mesopotamia predates the first written records and when the term Dilmun first appeared it was probably being used to describe anything lying south of the Shatt al Arab, including the Eastern Province of Arabia and perhaps even copper-producing Oman. Later, in the third millennium, it was applied to the Eastern Province, and to the Bahrain islands, and eventually to Failaka as well. The changes in the nomenclature probably reflect the state and accuracy of Mesopotamian geographical knowledge and the frequency of contacts. They may also reflect movements in the focus of power within Dilmun from the Eastern Province to Bahrain, and finally to Failaka, as the various internal political centres waxed and waned. In spite of all this change there are certain characteristics which remain constant. Dilmun always lay athwart the vital route linking southern Mesopotamia with the copper of Oman and the luxuries of the Indus valley; copper and timber were always the main commodities traded and the prosperity of Dilmun derived from this trade.

The Sumerian vision of Dilmun as a paradise land heavily influenced early studies of the archaeology of Bahrain. Taken in conjunction with the enormous numbers of burial mounds reported by the early European travellers, it encouraged a picture of the island as a huge necropolis to which people were brought to be buried in its sacred soil (most recently see Lamberg-Karlovsky 1986). The analogy was frequently drawn with the desire of the devout Shia Muslim to be buried in the sacred cities of Karbala and Najaf in southern Iraq. This interpretation was encouraged by an apparent lack of settlement sites contemporary with the burial mounds.

It is only in the last thirty years that settlement sites of the same date as the mounds have been positively identified by survey and excavation. More detailed studies have also shown that the burial mounds were built over a very long period of time, lasting into the Hellenistic age. It had previously been assumed that the vast majority belonged to the Dilmun period itself. These two new pieces of information demonstrate that there is no longer any need to postulate an influx of corpses from outside the island in order to account for the number of burials known. The newly identified towns and villages show that enough local people lived on the island to fill the graves which were built over a period of perhaps two thousand years. The graves should now be seen as the burial places of the islanders themselves throughout its long history and the idea of Bahrain as a necropolis can itself be buried.

Other myths have also accumulated around the islands of Bahrain. Early scholars, influenced mainly by the writings of Herodotus, regarded them as the homeland of the Phoenicians. This view is now also seen as fallacious, and little evidence can be produced to support it. (The evidence has been extensively reviewed by Bowersock in his 1986 article.)

Today, with more accurate evidence available to us, we are able to move towards a clearer picture of the history of Dilmun. We can begin to trace some of the fluctuations in its fortunes, to postulate the reasons for them, and to assess its significance in relation to its better known neighbours. The new data, available from excavations and scientific studies of many kinds on the material remains recovered from the excavations, taken in conjunction with textual evidence, underline the unique nature of the culture which emerged in the Arabian Gulf in the middle of the third millennium. In terms of its material culture Dilmun owed remarkably little to the great 'High Civilizations' with which it had important trading contacts and it quickly developed its own distinctive character. This book will attempt to trace this development, using, where appropriate, contemporary evidence from Mesopotamia, Iran, Oman and the Indus valley to try to understand the events described.

THE PHYSICAL SETTING

The first step in this process must be to look at the physical conditions in which these events took place. Greater Dilmun, by which is meant Eastern Arabia and the area from Failaka in the north to Bahrain in the south, lies in a desert region with a hot and humid climate. Temperatures in the summer months can reach well over 40° centigrade with 100 per cent humidity and more. The fundamental physical characteristics seem to have changed relatively little in the last 8,000 years or so with the exception of a number of important changes in sea level, which can be charted in outline, although local sequences differ and remain to be clarified (Delongeville and Sanlaville 1987). Generally speaking, in about 6000 BC the sea level was considerably higher than it is today. This seems to be true for the whole of the west side of the Gulf, although tectonic movements at its northern end mean that the pattern there is not always the same as it is in the latitude of Bahrain. It has been suggested that this is the time when Bahrain became separated from the Arabian mainland.

The high sea level in about 6000 BC was followed by a general transgression. The raised beaches representing this high level are marked, both on Bahrain, and in the Eastern Province, by sites belonging to a period contemporary with the Ubaid period of Mesopotamia. These would originally have been on the shore, which seems to have been about two metres above today's high tide mark. A second peak in sea levels can be seen in the first half of the third millennium, though this did not reach as far inland as the surviving Ubaid-related sites. It may have destroyed others lying further to seaward. At the Qala'at al Bahrain on the north coast of the island, excavators found third-millennium sherds of Umm-an-Nar type, under a layer of water-laid deposits which seem to have been laid down at this time (Højlund and Andersen 1994). This secondary high was again followed by a transgression which continued into the second millennium and which allowed large scale settlement on the low-lying island of Failaka for the first time. A smaller rise marked the middle of the second millennium, to be followed by a steady decline into the Hellenistic period to levels below those of today.

These changes in sea level do not seem to have been the result of major climatic changes nor of dramatic changes in the amount of precipitation. Even so, they almost certainly had a considerable effect, through hydrostatic pressure, on the availability of fresh water from the underground aquifers on which the region has always relied for its water supply and which are now seriously depleted (Larsen 1983b: 16–20). At periods when the sea level was higher than today there is some evidence to suggest that fresh water was accessible in areas such as the island of Dalma off the coast of Abu Dhabi, which today have no springs. An important Ubaid period settlement has been found on this island and is being explored by a team from the London University School of Oriental and African Studies (Dr Geoffrey King pers. comm.). The wider availability of springs may be explained by Masry's remark that 'The water table in the major underground aquifers of Eastern Arabia is shown to have very likely been affected by eustatic oscillations' (Masry 1974: 156).

It seems that during the Holocene, rainfall in the northern Gulf region has always been below the 300 mm per annum necessary for reliable rain-fed agriculture. Cultivation has only ever been possible in limited oasis areas with fresh water where simple irrigation techniques could be employed, but these oases were more extensive, at least on the Arabian mainland, until the late fifth to early fourth millennia. Larsen (1983b: 144–5) quotes evidence to show that there was an extensive lacustrine system, joined by small rivers in the Hofuf area which survived at least into the late Holocene. These more hospitable conditions certainly allowed for the development of one large village site of fourth-millennium date here (Adams *et al.* 1977 site 208/38). In addition to oasis cultivation, catch crops of cereals can be grown in wet years. On Bahrain people alive today recall cereals being grown south of the Rifaʿa ridge in the playa which developed north of the Jebel Dhokan. (See photographs in Yateem 1992: 90–1 of Shaikh Salman, the father of the present ruler, inspecting the wheat crop on the island, and of a harvest celebration in west Rifaʿa in the 1940s.) Such catch crops, by their nature, could not always be relied on to provide a major contribution to the diet.

The produce of the land may have been restricted by climatic conditions, but the sea provided a rich resource, with abundant fish and shellfish which could be fed to animals and humans. Fish and seaweed could also be used as fertiliser and fodder. In addition to the edible molluscs, shellfish offered other resources and pearl fishing has a long history in the Gulf. Pearls have been found on archaeological sites in the region from the Ubaid period onwards and fishbones usually outnumber the mammalian remains on archaeological sites. The land, however, was rich in non-agricultural resources. Copper from south-east Arabia was probably the most sought after commodity from the area, but stones such as flint, diorite, carnelian and a variety of softstones were also much prized and the sea was a vital link in distributing them. Before the advent of metalled roads and efficient wheeled transport, communications and the movement of heavy goods was far easier by water than by land. Such goods travelled north to Mesopotamia which lacked them all and it was control of the distribution networks which was the key to prosperity in the Gulf. It was its position across this major economic artery and its status as a port of trade, rather than its own natural resources, which gave Dilmun its wealth.

THE EASTERN PROVINCE

The Eastern Province is a long, thin, eastward-sloping coastal strip of territory stretching over 750 km. It is largely composed of marine terraces and salt flats overlying the rocky Arabian shield. A number of wide, shallow wadis with subterranean aquifers which water the two great oases of Qatif on the coast, and al Hasa inland to the south, run from the central highlands to the sea. Al Hasa is the larger of the two and covers approximately 180 sq. km of cultivated land. It is possible to grow cereals as well as date palms, fruit trees and a wide variety of vegetables in these areas. The wadis also provide access from the coast to central Arabia and its resources. These include deposits of softstone or chlorite which are said to lie south of Riyadh. Another important route lies to the north where the Wadi Batin has always been a major thoroughfare for groups travelling between Arabia and southern Mesopotamia. It has even been suggested that some of the earliest inhabitants of southern Mesopotamia may have entered the country by this route (Piesenger 1983). The Wadi Batin remained an important tribal migration route until the present century (*Naval Intelligence Iraq* 1944).

Although the configuration of the coastline must have changed considerably as the result of the changes in sea level referred to above, it seems safe to suggest that there were always a very limited number of good anchorages on this stretch of the Gulf. The bay east of Qatif and south of the important third-millennium island site of Tarut was probably one such harbour and retained its importance into the nineteenth century when the *Arabian Gulf Intelligence Manual* of 1856 described it as a safe anchorage for small boats (Fig. 1.3). Palgrave sailed from here to Bahrain in 1863 and the journey took three days (Palgrave 1883). The *Manual* also mentions a harbour a little further south at Uqair, fourteen miles from Bahrain and at the mouth of one of the important wadis giving access to the interior via al Hasa and Hofuf. There is no direct evidence for a Dilmun period site here, but it seems possible, given the distribution of sites in the interior, that one existed, linking Bahrain by the most direct route with the interior of Arabia.

Such harbours would have been vital links in the early communication networks. Some idea of the time needed to transport goods and people can be gained from ethnographic evidence dating to the period before motorized transport. A caravan travelling

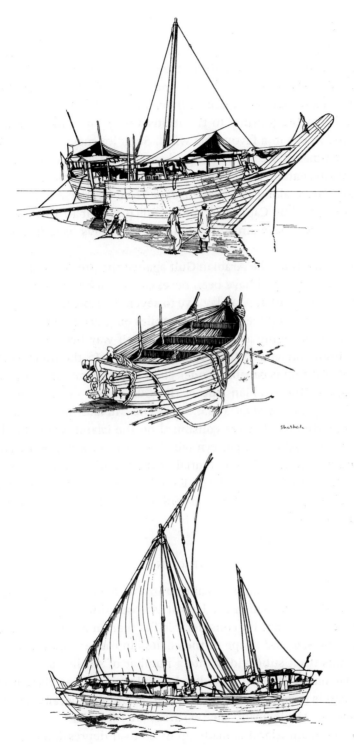

1.3 Boats from the Gulf region: a boum, a reed boat or shashak and a sambuk.

from the coast at Uqair took two days in 1856 to reach the oasis of al Hasa. From there it took a further four days to get to Qatif to the north. Going in the other direction, the journey from Uqair to Bahrain took a day, and that from Bahrain to Hormuz on the Iranian coast four more days (*Arabian Gulf Intelligence Manual* 1856). By analogy, it can be suggested that the journey to the Indus valley ports like Lothal might have taken two to three weeks in a favourable wind. Such journeys would only have been possible at certain times of the year, taking advantage of the prevailing north to north-west wind. As an alternative, if the conditions were unfavourable, there was also a reasonably easy land route along the coast of Iran from Bandar Abbas via the Makran coast which was mapped by Captain Grant in 1809 (Chakrabati 1990, map facing page 98). Heavy goods, as we have already noted, would always have travelled by sea for preference.

Travelling northwards up the Arabian Gulf against the prevailing north winds must have been slower and it would have been necessary to tack from shore to shore of the Gulf. The mouth of the Shatt al Arab lay five to seven days north of Bahrain. The value of Bahrain's position as a stopover for fresh supplies on journeys up and down the Gulf is immediately apparent, lying as it does roughly half way between the mouth of the great rivers of Mesopotamia and the straits of Hormuz. In the nineteenth century it was still said that 'Bahrain is capable, under good government, of being very valuable as the whole trade of the Arabian side of the Gulf might be centred in the island' (*Arabian Gulf Intelligence Manual* 1985: 567). The *Manual* noted that only about a quarter of the imported goods were consumed on the island, while the bulk was re-exported to other destinations, a pattern which seems to correspond well to what we see in the second millennium. The potential of the island is even greater than this as much trade from the Iranian side of the Gulf could also be funnelled through its ports. Even today, the dhow ports of Manama are full of boats from Iran and India carrying fresh produce and other goods.

BAHRAIN

It is time to look now at the islands of Bahrain in a little more detail. Today Bahrain is an archipelago of islands of which the largest is about thirty-five miles long and ten miles across. There is evidence for considerable fluctuation in the shoreline and so it is difficult to know the size and shape of the islands in earlier times. It is possible that the main island was itself subdivided into a number of smaller ones in the fifth millennium and that much of what is today low-lying land was then under the sea. Originally, the islands formed part of the Arabian massif and became separated from it in the early Holocene. Geologically the two areas are identical.

The centre of the main island is made up of an oval depression dominated by the limestone mass of the Jebel Dokhan which rises to 450 feet above sea level. North of this is an area rich in springs and potentially fertile, while to the south lies desert, home to gazelle and other wild animals. The rocky ridges of the main island are made of rather poor quality, porous limestone which was widely used for building. The better quality stone used to build the second great Barbar temple was brought in from the neighbouring island of Jiddah. Flint is also abundant and there is said to have been at least one pool of bitumen at Qars, south of the jebel (Lorimer 1970 II: 21 and 231). Bitumen was an extremely valuable commodity, as it was the only natural adhesive and waterproofing material known in antiquity and it is therefore puzzling that this source does not seem to have been used in antiquity (Conan 1996). In addition, Lorimer refers to salt pans at Mattala in the south-west of the island (Lorimer 1970 II: 214), an area now closed, but where tumuli are shown on old maps such as that printed by Glob (1968), suggesting that they may have been exploited in antiquity.

The coastline of the Bahrain islands is changing all the time. Today, this is the result of land reclamation schemes. In earlier times, as we saw above, it was due to the natural rise and fall of the sea level. At the time of the first settlements on the islands the sea was considerably higher than it is today. Since then there have been many fluctuations affecting the location of the harbours and of the settlements themselves. It seems clear, however, that from the third millennium onwards the main island boasted at least two safe harbours able to take sea-going boats and probably a number of other smaller anchorages where fishing boats could be beached in safety. Judging from the historical evidence, one harbour lay in the vicinity of the Qala'at al Bahrain, while the other was on the east coast, probably close to Tubli Bay, which may well have extended westwards from its present position towards the Saar ridge. It has been suggested that the inhabitants of the islands have been dredging and cutting channels through the coral reefs to improve access since very early times (Kervran 1988). These sheltered anchorages would have been as important as the supplies of fresh water in establishing Bahrain's position as a vital refuelling post on the long trade route down the Gulf towards the Indus valley.

The artesian springs on which the island has always relied for its survival lie mainly in the northern third of the island and down its west side. It is in these areas that settlement has always been concentrated, although a few villages also occur on the east coast. This pattern can still be seen on a modern map of Bahrain, even though much of the water is now supplied from desalinization plants and many of the aquifers have been contaminated. It is even more marked on maps showing the distribution of archaeological sites (see Larsen 1983b). The density of settlement has always been greatest on the northern coastal strip and down the west coast where the springs provide the greatest potential for agriculture. Carsten Niebuhr, writing in the eighteenth century, says the island had 365 villages, but Mrs Bent, writing in the nineteenth century, refers to a more modest fifty (Rice 1984).

As we have already seen intensive garden cultivation is possible in the vicinity of

1.4 Date garden cultivation.

the springs using simple irrigation techniques, while cereals were grown south of Rifaʿa in living memory. There is no conclusive evidence for elaborate *qanāt* systems in the Dilmun period, but the possibility cannot be entirely ruled out (see chapter 4). It was for its garden produce that Bahrain was especially famous in the nineteenth century, a tradition which can be traced back to texts of the third millennium which refer to dates and onions or garlic as Dilmun specialities. Archaeobotanical remains from the site of Saar, in the northwest of the island, indicate that wheat, barley and dates were being grown then (Nesbitt 1993). Contemporary evidence from Failaka island to the north suggests a similar range of crops (Calvet and Gachet 1990: 49). Evidence from the oasis of Hili in the United Arab Emirates raised the possibility that, in addition, sorghum, imported from Africa, was also being used, but this identification has been challenged. It has also been claimed that sorghum occurs at RH5, a site in Oman dating to the fifth millennium, but this identification has also been questioned and it is now thought to be a large grass called *Setaria* sp. (Potts 1994: 237 and 256). Potts has also suggested that sisyphus may been exploited both for human consumption and for animal fodder (1994: 236).

The date palm was the most important garden crop (Fig. 1.4). The date is probably native to the Arabian peninsula, but little is known of its wild progenitor and its original distribution as most of the uncultivated trees found today are feral rather than truly wild. The date palm is arguably one of the most useful plants known to man. Every part of it is utilized: the fruit is very nutritious with a high sugar content; the sap is also a sweetener and can be used to make a fermented drink; the stones can be used for charcoal or ground up to make animal fodder high in protein; the leaves are woven into mats used, amongst other things, to build the traditional *barasti* huts of the region; palm fibres can be twisted into rope, while the trunks provide timber for building and other purposes. In addition, the shade below the palms in the date gardens provides the perfect environment for growing fruit trees and tender plants of many kinds. The dates of Dilmun, as mentioned above, enjoyed an excellent reputation in ancient Mesopotamia and seem to have given their name to a particular variety which may have originated in the islands. We cannot, however, assume that Dilmun dates mentioned in the texts always came from Dilmun any more than today we can assume that sprouts come from Brussels or cabbages from Savoy.

Perhaps it was the sea itself which was Dilmun's most important resource. There are about 700 exploitable species of fish in the Gulf today. In the past fish provided the main source of protein in the diet of the inhabitants of the islands and were also used as a rich source of fertiliser. In addition they provided fodder for the animals. The Gulf is also rich in shellfish which were important as food, as bait, and for the pearls and mother-of-pearl they provided. Mother-of-pearl was widely used in Mesopotamia and Syria for inlay work in the third millennium. The column in the centre of certain shells could be used to make stamp and cylinder seals, or beads. The murex shell found in these waters is the source of a much prized purple dye, but there is only minimal evidence to suggest that it too may have been exploited in the Dilmun period. Fragments of wall plaster decorated with purple paint have been found in the temple at Saar and very large quantities of a similar shell called *Thais savignyi*, a member of the Muricacea family, were found at the site of Khor Ile-Sud in Qatar, where they were being processed in the somewhat later Kassite period (Edens 1994: 209–24).

These marine resources can be tapped in many different ways. The people of Dilmun had sea-going boats some of which, judging by the drawings on the stamp seals of the period, had central masts with sails and upturned prows (Fig. 1.5). Others were simpler and were rowed or poled, while others appear to have been made from bundles of reeds or palm fronds tied together. These boats could certainly have been used for both inshore and deep water fishing. Copper fish hooks from Dilmun sites show that these were used to catch certain types of fish. Although no evidence survives, it seems reasonable to guess that nets and traps were also commonly used, just as they are to this day. The great traps (Fig. 1.6) in the coastal waters of Bahrain today, when seen from the air, look like arrowheads in the sea.

The Arabian peninsula has always been characterized by a number of complementary subsistence strategies, farming, fishing and herding, as well as the hi-tech

1.5 A reed boat and a sailing boat depicted on seals of the Early Dilmun period.

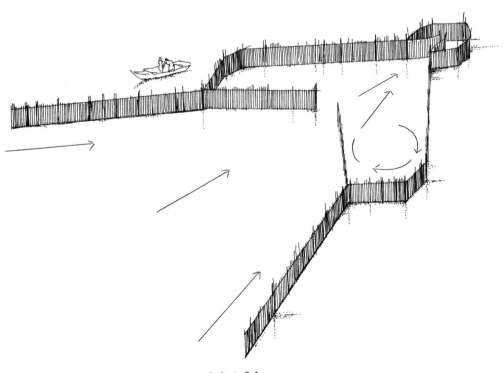

1.6 A fish trap.

modern industries often associated with oil. In the early second millennium for instance, it seems probable that fully urban settlements interacted with the smaller agricultural villages, specialized fishermen and the fulltime pastoralists who lived on the fringes of the cultivated areas just as they do today. Even the industrial component was present by the third millennium in the form of copper mines of the Oman peninsula. It was the range and flexibility of the subsistence strategies, coupled with its favourable geographical position on one of the major trade routes of the ancient world, which gave Dilmun the capacity to develop into a unique civilization and the resilience to survive in an inhospitable region.

This book will describe the material culture of what may perhaps be called Greater Dilmun, that is the region on the west coast of the Gulf from Failaka in the north to Bahrain in the south, from the coming of the first hunter-gatherers to use pottery, via the emergence of the urban centres, to its relapse into provincialism in the middle of the second millennium under the kings of the Kassite dynasty of Mesopotamia. Developments in the region will be contrasted with those to the south and south-east in Oman and the Emirates, ancient Magan, and an attempt will be made to show how the balance of economic power passed from one to the other. Interesting contrasts can also be drawn between the social organization in the two areas. For example, in the late third millennium the archaeological evidence from Oman suggests the presence of a non-urban, non-specialized society based on a chiefdom type political organization with the extended family as the basic building block of society. In the Eastern Province and Bahrain we have, it will be suggested, fully urban settlements first on Tarut island and then at the Qalaʿat al Bahrain. There is also evidence here for what appears to be a craft-specialized society with the nuclear family as the basic unit. Control of the trade routes seems to have passed between Dilmun and Magan for reasons which it is still impossible for us to identify with any certainty. Each of the two areas also developed its own distinctive material culture, owing remarkably little either to its immediate neighbours, or to the trading partners at either end of the trade routes. One striking illustration of this is the use in Dilmun of circular stamp seals with a specific iconography: in Oman very few seals of any kind have been found, although a recent find from Abraq suggests that a different sort of stamp seal may be native here (Potts 1993d: 434); in Mesopotamia cylinder seals were the standard form, while in the Indus valley the square stamp seal is the usual shape.

One especially intriguing question remains unanswered about the Dilmun civilization. We do not know whether it had a writing system. It was in contact with at least three literate civilizations, one in Mesopotamia, one in Susa and the third in the Indus valley; in addition, it should be remembered that writing seems to have emerged in the fourth millennium in response to the need to keep track of economic transactions of an increasingly complex nature (Nissen 1993). Such a need certainly existed in Dilmun, though it may have been met in other ways, but it is difficult to believe that the canny merchants of Dilmun did not see the benefits of developing some kind of recording system. Apart from a few signs from the Indus valley system of writing which are found on the so-called Persian Gulf seals, and a few cuneiform inscriptions, no other written evidence has survived from the islands. Solving this mystery is one of the goals of all archaeologists working in the Gulf region.

It has been suggested by experts who work on seals that stamp seals are better adapted to use with ink and paper or skins than with clay tablets. On the other hand, cylinder seals which can easily be rolled over large surface areas are ideal for use on clay. If this is correct, then the use of stamp seals in Dilmun may indicate that they wrote on some perishable material such as palm leaves or parchment, using inks or dyes from natural sources such as cuttlefish. We can only hope that they also erected monumental inscriptions on more permanent materials such as stone or our chances of finding documents must be very remote.

The lack of indigenous written sources is a serious handicap in any attempt to reconstruct the social, political and economic life of Dilmun, but we are very fortunate in having a certain amount of information in the cuneiform texts from Mesopotamia, Mari, and more recently, from Tell Mardikh in Syria, the ancient city of Ebla. There is also a rapidly increasing body of archaeological evidence, much of it excavated in the last ten years by teams from many nations. This archaeological activity is largely due to the enlightened attitude of governments in many of the states concerned. There is a growing pride and interest in the archaeological heritage. Protective legislation is in place, and local archaeologists are undertaking important work in rescue archaeology ahead of major development projects. The value of archaeology is appreciated for both its cultural and economic importance. The provision of a series of excellent new museums throughout the region serves as a source of national pride, an important educational resource and as a tourist attraction.

This new interest in the past and the enormous amount of new information available are the twin justifications for this book.

Chapter 2

THE EARLIEST SETTLEMENTS

The inhospitable nature of much of the Arabian peninsula has always meant that, in order to survive, people have had to rely on a variety of natural resources, and have had to be prepared to shift from one to the other as the vagaries of weather, and at a later date, of tribal politics demanded.

The first evidence for human activity in the Eastern Arabia has been retrieved from about forty archaeological sites yielding a wide variety of flint tools (Fig. 2.1), but no pottery. They seem to belong to a time when the great lakes of the early Holocene had not completely dried out and when water was more widely available than it is today. In spite of this, recent research has indicated that there are no true Palaeolithic sites here, or in Bahrain. Potts (1990: 32) states 'With the elimination of a Palaeolithic horizon in Eastern Arabia, the blade-arrowhead tradition (of flint tools) first identified as Group B in Qatar . . . becomes the earliest post-pleistocene archaeological component in the Arabian Gulf area.' This Group B flint assemblage should probably be dated to the eighth to sixth millennia BC and has some similarities to the earlier Pre-Pottery Neolithic B of Jordan, while types A, C and D are found into the fifth and early fourth millennia associated with Ubaid pottery at the sites of Khor, in Qatar (Inizan 1980), and al Markh on the island of Bahrain (Roaf 1976).

In all, four different tool assemblages have now been identified in Eastern Arabia in the pre-pottery phase, predominantly of flint, but with a number of obsidian blades and arrowheads (Nayeem 1992: 68 and Fig. XXI). These assemblages also occur in Qatar which seems to share the same material culture, though only C and D. (Larsen 1983b: 29 and Roaf 1976) are found on Bahrain. These assemblages were labelled A–D by Kapel who first defined them, and were arranged in a chronological/alphabetic sequence with A as the oldest (Kapel 1967). However, more recent research by a French team in Qatar has reassessed this sequence and has shown that, although Group B is the oldest, all four are in part contemporary (Tixier 1986; Potts 1990). Each group is dominated by a different type of tool: Group A has large hand axes and scrapers; Group B has blade tools; C has a different sort of scraper, while D has a wide variety of blades, tanged arrows and small tools all finished with pressure flaking. As the different types of tools are, broadly speaking, contemporary, it suggests that the differences in the assemblages are due to differences in function, rather than to successive stages of technological development. We are looking at tools used for a variety of different jobs, not at tools of widely differing dates (de Cardi 1986: 89).

19

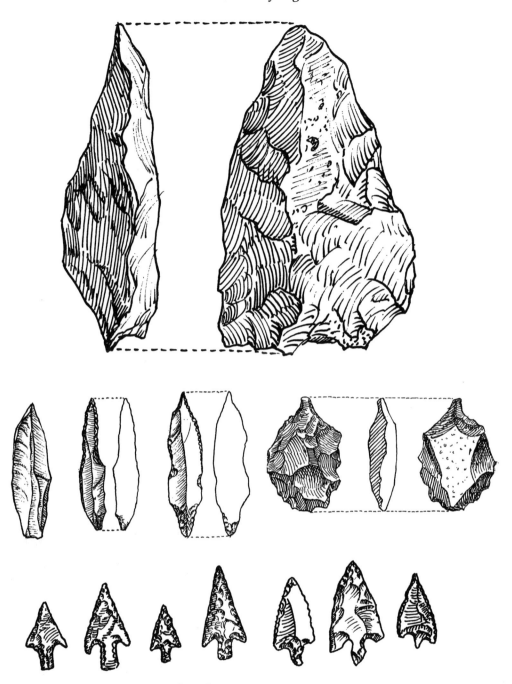

2.1 Flints from groups A, B, C and D.

The presence of four different, specialized, tool kits supports the suggestion made by Masry, amongst others (Masry 1974), that a number of different subsistence strategies can be identified in the region even at this early period in its history. There is little direct evidence, but the tools suggest that hunting was still important, as arrowheads and tools such as scrapers and choppers for preparing the carcasses are all present. Gazelle bones and the remains of other wild animals have also been found on some of the early sites and one site, Ain Qannas, may have been a specialist butchering site for equids (Masry 1974: 155). There is also some evidence for the presence of domesticated animals: the bones of domesticated cattle have been identified at the fifth-millennium site of Dosariyah, on the coast south of Jubail (Masry 1974: 166). Bones of sheep, goat and dog were also found here, but the remains were too fragmentary to be able to establish whether they were those of domesticated animals or not. It is clear from the cattle bones that some herding was already being practised in the fifth millennium so it can be suggested that the move towards agriculture and a more sedentary lifestyle may have already begun, thus providing a second subsistence strategy.

The cultivation of plants, as well as the herding of certain animals, may be suggested by seed impressions on coarse pottery at the same fifth-millennium site of Dosariyah on the central coastal strip, but the seeds could have been collected from wild plants. Heavy stone tools found at the same site may provide another pointer in the direction of cultivation as they may have been used as crude hoes, or as pounders for processing the seeds (Masry 1974: 168). None of the early cultivars such as wheat, barley, lentils, peas and flax are native to Arabia and this, together with the inhospitable, hot, dry climate, probably explains the relatively late appearance of agriculture in the peninsula. Cultivation would only have been possible in limited areas in the oases which were fed by underground aquifers and simple irrigation would probably also have been necessary to produce a significant source of food. The date palm is the only cultivar which is native to the region and it may well have been exploited at an early stage, although the fruit of the wild species is said to have small fruit which are 'non-palatable and even indigestible' (Zohary and Hopf 1994: 158).

There is also evidence for an important and successful subsistence strategy based on the sea as fish, shellfish and the remains of sea mammals are all found on almost all sites of this date, even inland. These different survival strategies were complementary and the same people may have used several simultaneously or in sequence, as circumstances demanded. Other natural resources of great value to the early inhabitants such as flint, salt and clay are available in different parts of the region and may have been exploited by both mobile hunter-gatherers and the more sedentary inhabitants based in some of the larger communities for which we have evidence from the fifth millennium onwards. Goods were also probably exchanged between the groups of people practising the different strategies in different parts of the region. Sea shells and fishbone have been found far inland at the site of Ain Qannas in the al Hasa oasis and could represent such an exchange.

The evidence for climatic fluctuations and progressive desiccation, such as that provided by the changing water level in the spring at the fifth-millennium site of Ain Qannas, would have made a variety of subsistence strategies even more desirable, if not essential, for the survival of the community. This flexibility, provided by the ability to shift from hunting to stock herding, to fishing or fullblown agriculture is still visible in the pattern of interlocking economies which was commonplace until recently all around the shores of the Gulf.

For example, in the *Arabian Gulf Intelligence Manual* of 1856 the Shihiyyin tribe is described as being split in two, one section living in the coastal towns such as Julfar and being active in pearl fishing, trade and agriculture while the other wandered the country with their flocks or eked out a precarious living by fishing. The same source also describes the Beniyas as being divided into three, some of whom were camel or cattle herders, some fishermen and pearl fishers, while some cultivated date gardens. The human mobility necessitated by this economic flexibility was made possible by a shifting and complicated network of financial and kinship ties which brought with them reciprocal obligations. These ties linked settled and nomadic groups, villagers, fishermen and townspeople, many of whom belonged to the same extended families or tribal groupings. A similar economic flexibility is discussed in a totally different environment by Cribb in his study of the pastoral nomads of Eastern Turkey. He states that '"nomadic" and "sedentary" sectors of the community are actually interchangeable.' (Cribb 1991: 25).

The intrinsic nature of the country and the distribution of early sites on the ground, together with the evidence from them for a variety of subsistence strategies, strongly suggests that a similar pattern can be projected back into the earliest periods. This evidence has been most thoroughly explored in the Eastern Province where Masry (1974) has studied about forty sites and more recently McClure and al-Shaikh have reported in some detail on five more (McClure 1993). Some of these sites are fishermen's camps on the coast, while one or two seem to be more substantial settlements with the remains of solid buildings of *farush*. In one case the remains of imported bitumen were found (McClure 1993: 115). There must be some doubt about the date of some of these buildings as later material has also been found at the sites concerned. Other settlements are no more than small scatters of flints near outcrops from which the raw material could be collected and shaped for easy transport. Four of the sites identified by Masry and McClure stand out by virtue of their size and are considerable mounds, two of them more than three metres high, lying in oases where irrigation agriculture is practicable with minimum effort. Each of these larger sites is surrounded by a dispersed pattern of small, probably temporary, seasonal or special purpose sites (Fig. 2.2). These may represent butchery or hunting camps and the flint processing sites already mentioned. We are already looking at what the geographers call a two-tier settlement pattern, with

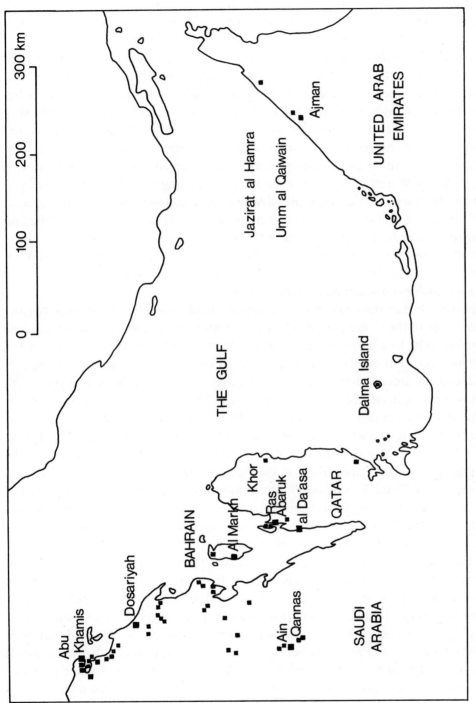

2.2 Map of the main sites in the Gulf where Ubaid pottery has been found.

some differentiation visible between the two tiers. The smaller specialist sites probably supplied raw materials and even partly processed goods to the larger ones which,
it can be suggested, offered various goods and services in return.

Three of the four mound sites referred to above, are linked by the occurrence at each
of them of the earliest pottery found in Arabia. Surprisingly, this pottery can be identified as the ware known in southern Mesopotamia as Ubaid. Analysis of the rather
greenish fabric from which much of it is made showed that it had originated in the silty
Mesopotamian plain and was not a local imitation (Roaf 1994). The designs are painted
in a purplish paint and frequently consist of no more than a few wavy lines, although
the earliest sherds show much denser, more tightly packed designs of small squares
(Fig. 2.3). Many sherds have lost their decoration through erosion. This pottery is
widely distributed down the east coast of Arabia and is found from Kuwait to the coast
of the Emirates, as well as on the main island of Bahrain. It has also been identified on
the Iranian coast at Bushire (Oates 1986: 84). The Ubaid pottery is found with a coarse
red pot which seems to be locally made and a finer red ware of uncertain origin. Flint
tools in the native tradition are found in the same contexts. This gives us a means of
dating such tools even when no pottery is present.

It is possible to date the Arabian sites on which Ubaid pottery has been found to more
than one phase of the Ubaid period. The Ubaid pottery of Mesopotamia was traditionally divided on stylistic grounds into four closely related phases, labelled by Oates 1–4
(Oates 1960). Not all these styles are sequential. There is some evidence to suggest that
Ubaid 2 had no independent chronological existence, but overlapped in time with
Ubaid 1 on the one hand and Ubaid 3 on the other. The sequence at Eridu for example,
would tend to support this view and even at the type site for Ubaid 2 at Ras al Amiya,
this ware is always found with either the earlier or the later wares (Safar and Lloyd 1981;
Stronach 1961). Recently an even earlier stage, called Ubaid 0, has been isolated at the
site of Oueili in southern Iraq (Huot in Henrickson 1989), and a post-Ubaid horizon,
sometimes called Ubaid 5, is also recognized at Oueili and at Ur and Uruk, where it
marks the transition to the plain wares typical of the succeeding Uruk period (Oates
1984: 260). No Ubaid 0 or 1 wares have yet been found in the Gulf. The earliest evidence
for contacts with Mesopotamia comes from examples of Ubaid 2 and 3 wares found on
the Iranian coast near Bushire (Oates 1986), at Dosariyah on the central coastal strip and
at Ain Qannas in the al Hasa oasis (Masry 1974). It was also recognized at a number of
smaller sites in the same areas. The distribution of this pottery predominantly along the
coast strongly suggests that contact with Mesopotamia was by sea with boats 'coast-
hopping' from one water source or local settlement to another. Goods could then have
been disseminated inland along the wadis to sites like Ain Qannas, as they are today. If
the contacts had been by land, via the Wadi Batin for example, a very different distribution would be seen with sites clumped in the north. At least two Ubaid-period sites
have also been reported from mainland Kuwait (Zarins 1992: 68).

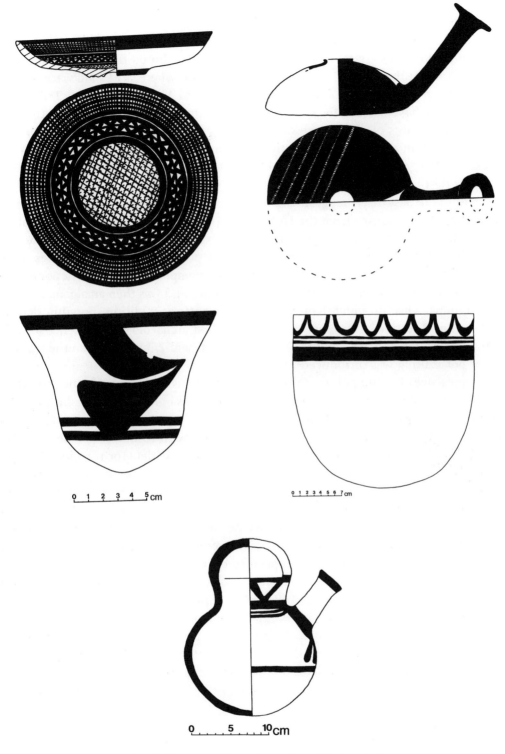

2.3 Ubaid pottery from phases 1–4 of that period.

Later Ubaid wares are found even more widely distributed from Kuwait and Abu Khamis to al Markh on Bahrain and as far south as Qatar where late Ubaid ware is found at al Daʿasa on the west coast and at a number of sites in Abu Dhabi close to Tell Abraq. Ubaid pottery has also been found in Umm-al-Qawain and Ras al Khaimah (Potts 1990: 53–4). The amounts of pottery are small and suggest that the contacts may well have been intermittent and of little economic importance. The fact that the pottery is sometimes found in graves suggests that it, or its contents, may have had an ideological significance for the inhabitants of these settlements.

It has, in the past, been suggested that the earliest inhabitants of Mesopotamia may have entered the country from the Gulf region (Piesinger 1983). This is now looking increasingly unlikely as there is no trace of the Ubaid 0 wares used by the first settlers in southern Mesopotamia in the Gulf; the earliest pottery from the Gulf dates to the Ubaid 2/3 phase. It is of course, possible that some component of the early population of southern Mesopotamia did originate further south and was then amalgamated with other groups, some of which had a pre-existing pottery tradition, possibly derived from Iran or Palestine. At present, however, the first archaeological evidence for contacts between Mesopotamia and the Gulf is in the Ubaid 2/3 phase when the technology of pot-making was introduced to Arabia.

The presence of Ubaid pottery in the Gulf provides us with evidence for absolute as well as relative dates. Carbon 14 dates from Ubaid levels in Mesopotamia show that the Ubaid period covered most of the fifth millennium. Greater precision is difficult to achieve as the interpretation of these dates is beset with technical problems. It is a period when massive corrections are necessary to the raw data for reasons which are still unclear and sequences of dates from stratified deposits are rare (Aurenche *et al.* 1987). A number of C14 dates are also available from sites in the Eastern Province, but these too have their problems. Most of them were taken some time ago, they were calculated on the old Libby half life[1] and have not been corrected. In addition, many of them are derived from shell, a material which presents particular technical problems.

All the dates quoted below, unless specified otherwise, are taken from Masry 1974. Earliest uncorrected dates come from the middle, aceramic levels at the site of Ain Qannas which give dates of 4705 and 4935 BC, and predate the appearance of the short-lived levels containing Ubaid 2/3 ware.[2] The dates from Dosariyah, one of the Gulf sites with the longest occupation sequence, span almost the whole of the fifth millennium, with the oldest date at 4950 BC and the youngest, associated with Ubaid 2/3 pottery, at 4185 BC.[3] These two sets of dates do not agree very well, those from Dosariyah for the Ubaid 2/3 levels are rather lower than might be expected, while those from Ain

---

[1] For the new half life of C14 see Aitkin 1990.

[2] Potts gives corrected dates with a range between 6250 and 5220 BC which seems possible for the pre-pottery levels.

[3] Pott's corrected dates range from 5250–4935 BC for those deposits just below the surface to 6275–5340 BC from the lowest level reached. The lower end of the range seems preferable in each case.

Qannas agree better with the Mesopotamian evidence. Dates from Abu Khamis, where the pottery is described as middle to late Ubaid, of 3800 and 3615 BC, when crudely corrected give a middle to late fourth millennium date as could be expected from the Mesopotamian material.[4] It would seem then, that contacts with Mesopotamia were initiated sometime in the middle of the fifth millennium and may have continued into the fourth millennium, on the basis of the evidence from al Markh (see p. 31).

Interesting questions are now being asked about how the Mesopotamian pottery came to Arabia. Two possibilities have been hotly debated over the years since the first Ubaid pottery was identified in Arabia. Some scholars (e.g. Oates *et al.* 1977; Oates 1984) favour trade between a technologically slightly more advanced Mesopotamia and neighbouring Arabia through the agency of 'seafaring merchants' from the former. This phrase was first used by Oppenheim in a famous article relating to a period about 2,000 years later (Oppenheim 1954). Others (cf. Masry 1974) prefer to see the relationship as one of 'interaction spheres' characterized by the exchange of goods for ritual and prestige purposes between equals. Masry refers specifically to the exchange of the painted pottery, or its contents, for pearls and sea shells.

Other goods were probably involved too, such as bitumen, which McClure refers to from his Ubaid-related Site C south of Dhahran (McClure 1993), and which has also been found in Abu Dhabi at the contemporary Site 2 close to Tell Abraq by Carl Phillips (pers. comm.). The nearest major sources of bitumen are at Hit on the middle Euphrates, or in south-west Iran, although small springs are known from Kuwait and Bahrain (Lorimer 1970 II: 21 and 231). A limited amount of obsidian, another exotic material, has been found in the Eastern Province and in Bahrain, and appears to have originated in Eastern Anatolia, presumably travelling via Mesopotamia to its ultimate destination (Renfrew and Dixon: 1976). Obsidian is also known to occur in south-west Arabia, but these sources do not seem to have been exploited by the people from the Eastern Province at this early period (Zarins 1990). Even dates may have been exchanged, as the earliest remains of dates from southern Iraq have been found in late Ubaid levels at Tell Oueili and Eridu. It is not known if the wild date is native to Iraq, but it does seem to have been native to Arabia and may have travelled north from there (see chapter 1).

The dichotomy between these two exchange mechanisms is not as great as may appear at first sight. It seems possible that both may have been used. We can suggest that some of the Ubaid pottery was brought by people from southern Iraq and traded with groups living on the coast of Arabia such as that at Carl Phillips' Site 2. Here the burials of about forty people of all ages and both sexes show clearly that we are looking at a group of local inhabitants and not at a boatload of sailors engaged in a foraging expedition, who left their rubbish and their casualties behind. In addition, the burials

---

[4] Potts gives two ranges for this site, 4445–3870 BC and 4735–4380 BC, corrected.

at Site 2 are all crouched suggesting a local tradition, as the few Ubaid burials we know from southern Mesopotamia are extended (Safar and Lloyd 1981). From coastal sites like this and the ones at Abu Khamis etc. the pottery and other goods could subsequently be exchanged along the complex network of economic and social ties which, it has already been suggested, linked the coastal and inland areas via the great wadis. These links formed the type of interaction spheres referred to by Masry, but here the spheres link the coastal and inland inhabitants of Arabia.

The impact of the contacts with Mesopotamia was limited. The technology of potmaking was briefly adopted and a poor quality chaff-tempered red ware was produced which is found together with the imported Ubaid wares. Then, it is suggested, the skill was lost again and many sites, notably the larger ones, were deserted. We should, perhaps, be a little cautious about accepting this interpretation uncritically, as the dating of sites with only undecorated coarse wares, or no pottery at all, is notoriously difficult. Some of these sites may, in reality, postdate the Ubaid period at least in their latest phases. The evidence from the Ubaid period site of al Markh on Bahrain (Roaf 1994) supports this suggestion, as this site continued in use after the Ubaid contacts ceased. Minimal use of coarse pottery also continued so the skill does not seem to have disappeared entirely (Roaf 1994: 151.) There is also an interesting change in the economic base at al Markh as the bones of domesticated goats appear for the first time in the post-Ubaid levels.

De Cardi has already considered this possibility and suggests that some aceramic sites on the mainland may also postdate the Ubaid phase (de Cardi 1986: 90). If in the future, it can be shown that some of these sites do, indeed, date to a period immediately after the Ubaid contacts ceased, it would make the conventional view that there are no settlements of immediately post-Ubaid date in the Eastern Province something of a mirage. This would also have two further corollaries; that there was no break in the sequence of sedentary or semi-sedentary human occupation in the region and that, therefore, the known sites cover a longer timespan than originally proposed. This in turn implies that the settlement density at any given time was even lower than has previously been suggested.

THE UBAID-RELATED SITES IN THE EASTERN PROVINCE AND BAHRAIN

The best evidence we have for reconstructing the local way of life comes from the three largest tell sites in the Eastern Province, Abu Khamis, Dosariyah and Ain Qannas, but even here the picture is far from clear and more evidence is badly needed. We have seen how a variety of subsistence strategies were in use: the faunal evidence from Dosariyah suggests the herding of cattle, and possibly of sheep and goat as well; the seed impressions on pottery from the same site may point to the beginnings of agriculture; and the abundant remains of wild equid teeth at Ain Qannas, north of Hofuf, illustrate the continued importance of hunting. At Abu Khamis, on the coast, it is unsurprising that there is an overwhelming preponderance of marine fauna.[5]

The most northerly of the Ubaid-related tell sites to be described is Abu Khamis, also on the coast, where the economy was undoubtedly marine based. Fishbone makes up 85 per cent by weight of the bones recovered and large amounts of shell were also found. The tool kit is dominated by microlithic tools, drills and borers which, taken with the large numbers of pearl oysters, has led to the suggestion of an industry based on pearls and mother-of-pearl. Lime plaster suggests that the buildings were similar to those at Dosariyah and the range of pottery is also similar to Ubaid 3/4, red and coarse wares found. The coarse wares are again probably of local manufacture. The presence of Ubaid 4 wares at this site suggests that it continued in use longer than the other sites described above. There are a number of good sources of clay (and flint) close to the site. A new feature is the occurrence of spindle whorls, which would give further weight to the suggestion that sheep and goat were domesticated by this time.

The site of Dosariyah, lying on the central coastal strip, covers a total area of about 1.6 km with a shell mound three metres high in the centre. The sequence of deposits is interrupted by two sterile layers indicating that occupation was not continuous. Evidence for structures is confined to lime plaster fragments, some painted black, with reed or palm frond impressions on them, suggesting that they came from the walls of *barasti*-type huts. The pottery is again a mixture of Ubaid 2/3 and red wares, and here the red wares also show signs of painted decoration and of a cream slip. We know nothing of the origins of this red ware, it may be of local origin or it may be another import, perhaps from Iran. A painted red ware is reported from Bushire on the Iranian coast by Pézard (Pézard 1914). In addition to these two good quality wares, there are also a number of large coarse ware storage jars with a heavy straw temper and the impressions of seeds in the fabric. These are very probably of local manufacture as they would have been difficult to transport.

Tools from the site include heavy stone pounders or hoes and, together with the storage jars, they provide some support for the suggestion that cereals were being processed. Animal bones from Dosariyah are too few to allow firm conclusions to be drawn on their status, but sheep, goat and cattle are present in addition to gazelle and large amounts of fish. Obsidian blades were also found in some quantity, together with exotic stones, some used for tools and some for beads, and all implying again the presence of a far flung network of contacts linking these sites with Anatolia, Mesopotamia and Iran.

Little is known of the structure of these settlements as we do not have large horizontal exposures from any of them and the architectural remains are also very limited. At Ain Qannas, lying on the edge of a fossil lake in the al Hasa oasis, a sequence of

[5] Unless otherwise stated all the information on the Ubaid-related sites in the Eastern Province comes from Masry 1974.

fifteen levels was identified. Stone was used for building in the top four phases when the whole mound was also enclosed by a light structure made of organic materials. (Pottery was only found in these four levels.) Inside the enclosure was a smaller, circular wall of stones about ten metres in diameter. These stones may have been used to weigh down the edges of a tent, or, it has been suggested that they could be the remains of a *tholos* type building. The diameter is rather large for a *tholos*, most of those found in Mesopotamia are in the region of five metres in diameter, although larger ones are known (for example Mallowan and Rose 1935; for smaller versions see Akkermans 1993). If the stones are the remains of a *tholos* then the construction displays considerable engineering skills for which there is no other contemporary evidence. It is tempting to see this complex on the basis of size, as the home of a single family unit engaged, perhaps on a seasonal basis, in the hunting of wild equids. The outer structure may be the remains of a corral for the sheep, goat and cattle whose bones were recovered from the site. Unfortunately, the condition of the bones makes it impossible to say whether or not they were domesticated.

The earlier levels at this site have not yielded any structures, although a well was found in levels 6–14 which are aceramic. Level 5 then seems to mark a period without human occupation and levels 4–1 have yielded both Ubaid 2/3 wares and a good quality, light red plain ware of unknown origin. Exotic materials are represented by fragments of obsidian and sea shells and their presence here and at smaller sites such as Ain Dar, another Ubaid site in the Abqaiq area seventy-five kilometres from the coast, are good evidence of the sort of interlocking interaction spheres already discussed.

Obsidian does not occur in the Eastern Province and the one piece which has been analysed proved to have originated in Eastern Anatolia around Lake Van. This piece was found at Dhahran, but, unfortunately, its date is uncertain and it may come from a later, third-millennium context (Renfrew and Dixon 1976). The presence of Vannic obsidian in Arabia can probably best be explained as a long chain of exchanges in so-called 'Down the line' trade with the sailors from southern Mesopotamia supplying the last link in the chain.

In addition to these larger sites, there are a much greater number of small, camping or special purpose sites which lie in their vicinity and provide them with raw materials. A second smaller unexcavated site lies forty-five kilometres from Dosariyah at Khursaniyah, and a number of small sites are found associated with sources of flint and clay around all three of the major tell sites. As detailed survey work continues, more of these sites will doubtless be found, although deflation by wind and water and the redeposition of windblown sand probably mean that much evidence has gone for ever. In addition to these mainland sites Ubaid pottery also occurs on one or two of the offshore islands of the United Arab Emirates, including Dalma where a very substantial settlement site has been identified (Flavin and Shepherd 1994).

The new survey by McClure and al-Shaikh of an area just south of Dhahran (1993), shows how many sites are waiting to be discovered and has added a few new scraps of information to this cloudy picture. Five sites were identified running approximately west from the old coastline. At Site B the remains of a large building of *farush* blocks with plaster on the interior were identified, but its dating is not entirely clear. Another sizeable building was found at Site D, also of *farush*, but the fragments of alabaster vessels and of copper implements from this site must mean that a later date cannot be ruled out for this building either. Site C has yielded a considerable amount of pottery coated with bitumen and flat bitumen fragments impressed with a woven reed pattern, other pieces are impressed with a coarse woven fabric. The site is dated to the Ubaid on the basis of the presence of a simple painted sherd and both pink and red wares. A goblet with a solid foot in a brown ware also occurs and recalls the pottery found on Bahrain in the foundations of the first Barbar temple (Mus. cat.:14 nos. 3–9). If this comparison is valid, this site may also have been inhabited in the third millennium.

Carbon 14 dates with a range of 4320–4430 BC, uncalibrated, have been obtained for the ancient shoreline on which Site F stands and so provides *terminus post quem* for the sites themselves. The pottery is difficult to attribute to any specific phase within the Ubaid period because of its condition and some sherds are certainly of post-Ubaid date. The presence in bulk of imported bitumen is the most significant new piece of information from these sites, providing as it does more evidence for the international contacts of the people living here. If the sites also prove to have been used in the third millennium as well, they will begin to fill what has been seen as a surprising gap in the archaeological record.

Finally, the site of al Markh on Bahrain should also be described in a little more detail. Although still not fully published, it seems, in its first phase, to be a fishermen's camp, lying on a small island. The early phase of the site produced a limited range of late Ubaid pottery, some of which is said to be of Ubaid 5 date. It was then deserted and re-used in post-Ubaid times when sheep and goat seem to have been introduced. A very small amount of plain pottery continues in use during this second phase of occupation. There are also said to be flints of the C and D groups and fragments of basalt mortars and querns, suggesting the processing of seeds (Roaf 1994).

In summary, it seems that the earliest evidence for a human presence in the Eastern Province is provided by the B group flints, which probably date back to the seventh and sixth millennia and which continue in use into the fifth. At this time the tool kit diversifies and three new groups of flint types can be identified – A, C and D – each of which seems to have been adapted for a different subsistence strategy. All four groups were in use simultaneously and point to the complementary nature of the strategies necessary to survive in a difficult environment. The first evidence for herding, and perhaps for agriculture, comes from the middle of the fifth millennium, and hunting and especially fishing continue to be important sources of protein and of other raw materials. Other materials such as salt, clay and flint are found in the Eastern Province, although they are not evenly distributed across the terrain. This unequal distribution makes it unsurprising that we can already distinguish evidence for exchange and for a two-tier settlement pattern in which it seems probable that the larger centres acted as redistribution centres for these goods.

It is also from these sites that we have the best evidence for contacts between Arabia and the rest of the ancient world, contacts which were probably based on barter. Obsidian apparently came from Anatolia, passing through Mesopotamia en route; pottery which certainly originated in southern Mesopotamia in the middle to late Ubaid period is also found; a red ware whose origin is unknown is present; 'technology transfer' resulted in the production of a local coarse ware; and bitumen, possibly of Iranian or Iraqi origin, is also found. The imported pottery and other goods seem to have been redistributed from coastal sites like Dosariyah to those in the great inland oases, for instance Ain Qannas. Evidence for the social organization of the time is non-existent, but the very lack of it suggests a loose, egalitarian, kin-based structure for which parallels can be found in recent times.

QATAR

Survey work under the direction of Beatrice de Cardi in 1973 demonstrated that Ubaid pottery was present at a number of coastal sites here too, notably at al Da'asa where some pottery of Ubaid 2/3 type was found, although most of the sherds were later in date. Some from Ras Abaruk may be of Ubaid 5 type and are similar to pottery found at al Markh (Oates 1978). The flints from these sites are identical with those from sites in the Eastern Province at which Ubaid pot has been found and the same type of red ware also occurs. The contacts and economies of the sites in the two areas seem to have been identical. A number of cairn burials were also excavated, but proved impossible to date.

FOURTH MILLENNIUM EVIDENCE IN THE EASTERN PROVINCE AND BAHRAIN

It has been stated in the past that Eastern Arabia was largely deserted in the post-Ubaid phase, but as we have already seen the evidence from al Markh suggests that some sparse settlement may have continued. It is, however, clear that the major tell sites were all deserted, although McClure's Site D, and perhaps C too, appear to have continued in use. Two reasons have been put forward for this dramatic drop in the number of settlements; the first is that progressive desiccation dried out the springs and lakes in use in the Ubaid period, making permanent settlement impossible and forcing people to return to a nomadic lifestyle or to migrate. The second suggests that the desiccation led to a drop in sea level as a result of which the settlements

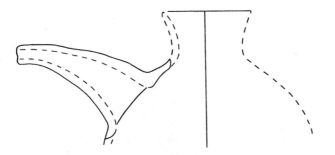

2.4 An Uruk-type spout from the Eastern Province.

moved down to the new shoreline. When the sea rose again, as it did in the fourth to early third millennia, the evidence for these sites was wiped out. These explanations both fail to explain the lack of settlements in the heart of the great oases and there is no convincing geophysical evidence to support the theory of catastrophic desiccation.

The true explanation may well be much less dramatic and require us to redate some of the aceramic sites and those with coarse ware to the post-Ubaid period as de Cardi has already suggested. There may also have been minor fluctuations in climatic conditions leading to some changes in the environment. We must also remember that parts of the Eastern Province are still virtually unsurveyed and much new evidence almost certainly remains to be found as McClure's 1993 survey shows. Archaeology in this area is still in its infancy. Even so, the desertion of the Ubaid-related tell sites requires an explanation which at the moment can only be guessed at.[6]

Evidence for the early part of the fourth millennium is very sparse, even if some of the aceramic sites are redated to the post-Ubaid period, and there is none for contacts with the outside world. By the second half of the millennium the position improves a little and some pottery of Uruk type is found from the Kuwaiti island of Qurain (Potts 1986a) to the Hofuf area (Fig. 2.4). None has yet been positively identified from Bahrain[7] (Larsen 1983b: 145–6; and more recently Zarins 1989). The bulk of Uruk pottery comes from the central area around Dhahran, while Piesinger's survey identified a number of sites with Uruk pottery in the Abqaiq area and at Umm-an-Nussi on the southern edge of the Jabrin oasis (Piesinger 1983). A clay bulla or envelope was also found at Dhahran and X-ray photographs showed that it contains a number of geometric tokens (Fig. 2.5). Such bullae are typical of the Uruk period in Mesopotamia, although they also occasionally occur later, and are normally connected

[6] It seems too, that the tell sites were not all abandoned at the same time; the pottery at Abu Khamis is said to include some 'late' Ubaid pottery as well as the Ubaid 2/3 wares.
[7] However, the author has seen a sherd of fine grey ware with a small beak lug which was picked up just north of the Early Dilmun site of Saar and which appeared to be Uruk in date.

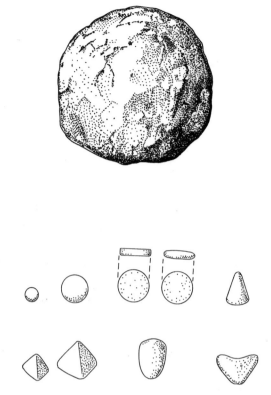

2.5 A bulla and tokens similar to those found in Dhahran.

with the recording of economic transactions, which makes its discovery in this context especially interesting (Schmandt-Besserat 1980). We do not know what the locally-made pottery, if it existed, was like at this period and we have no information on settlement type or settlement pattern.

The skimpy nature of the evidence suggests that the ties between Arabia and Mesopotamia were not close at this time. This may be explained by the evidence for an increasingly close and complex relationship between the alluvium and Central Anatolia on the one hand, and Khuzestan and highland Iran on the other. The evidence of settlements of various sorts along the major land and river routes to the north and east represents the remains of a farflung network of 'colonies and outposts' which supplied southern Mesopotamia with the raw materials which were almost entirely lacking on the plain from the middle Uruk period onwards (Algaze 1993). The impetus for contacts with Arabia was lacking in such circumstances and it is only with the collapse of this system in the latter part of the millennium that Mesopotamian pottery begins to appear in Eastern Arabia again in slightly greater quantities.

LATE FOURTH-MILLENNIUM EVIDENCE FROM THE OMAN PENINSULA

The evidence from the Oman peninsula complements that from Eastern Arabia. As we have already noted, copper was probably one of the most important commodities imported into southern Mesopotamia from Anatolia during the Uruk period and it seems to have become an essential component of the Mesopotamian economy. When the network collapsed it became necessary to find new sources which seem to have been in Oman. It is in the immediately post-Uruk period that the first references to Dilmun appear in the texts from level III of the Eanna complex at the great southern city of Uruk. These texts include a list of metal objects which refer to Dilmun axes, while other tablets record garments and various types of textiles which were allocated to people from Dilmun. The distribution of archaeological evidence for these contacts suggests that, at this time, Dilmun referred to a wide area from the Eastern Province to Oman (see chapter 1).

By the beginning of the third millennium the amount of evidence increases greatly and suggests a marked increase in the contacts between the two areas. The bulk of the evidence comes from Oman, rather than from the Eastern Province and strengthens the suggestion that the increased contact reflects the breakdown in the copper supply routes into Anatolia in the late Uruk period as the finds are clustered along the routes to the copper mines of the Hajar mountains. So-called Jemdat Nasr pots (Fig. 2.6), which belong to the last years of the fourth and the first years of the third millennia, have been found in a large number of stone-built graves in the United Arab Emirates and Oman (cf. chapter 6). These pots typically have short upright necks and everted rims, the upper body is decorated with polychrome geometric designs, divided into metopes, and the body is washed with a distinctive purple slip. The stone built graves are strung out along the routes which link the coast near Abu Dhabi itself with the interior, through modern trading centres like Ibri and Bat, before reaching as far south as Maysar. These areas are all rich in copper and other minerals as well as in exotic stones like steatite/chlorite which became very popular for certain types of vase in the middle of the third millennium (Frifelt 1975a). Frifelt reported that of about fifty graves excavated by her team, half contained Jemdat Nasr pottery. Locally made pottery also occurs together with other non-diagnostic goods which, Frifelt has tried to show, also have Mesopotamian parallels. The similarities are too generalized to be completely convincing (Frifelt in Alster 1983).

Finds of Jemdat Nasr pottery are rare in the Eastern Province itself and only a single sherd of plum-coloured ware is reported from Bahrain (Mortensen 1970: 395). It is said to have come from the Barbar temple site. However, the plum-coloured paint is very fugitive and there are at least two jars in the Bahrain National Museum which are identical in form to the ones from Oman, even though they now show no traces of paint (Vine 1993). In addition, a recut Jemdat Nasr seal was found in a grave at the al Hajjar

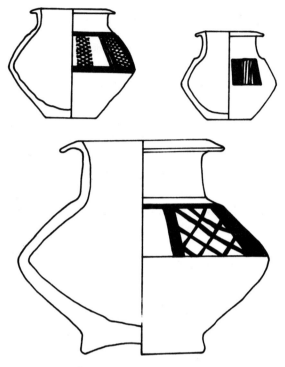

2.6 Jemdat Nasr pottery from Arabia.

site on Bahrain, but we do not know when it was recut and it may not have arrived on the island until after this recutting (Rice 1972).

The lack of any evidence for settlement and the very meagre nature of the finds means that it is impossible to determine what the nature of these contacts may have been. We cannot even tell if the contact was a direct one between traders from southern Mesopotamia and the copper producers of the interior of the Oman peninsula, or whether middlemen of some sort were involved, perhaps bringing the copper from the interior as far as the coast where the exchange could take place. The goods exchanged presumably included the pottery jars and their contents which could then be redistributed to the producers along the route described above. By the middle of the third millennium the island of Umm-an-Nar seems to have been such an entrepot, but as yet there is no evidence for an earlier centre. It is also possible that the important trading centre at Tarut was already in existence and may have played a part in the trade.

Any conclusions drawn have to remain speculative until the quality and quantity of the evidence from the middle of the third millennium increases. The contacts, whatever their nature, seem largely to have bypassed the Eastern Province and the Bahrain islands in the early fourth millennium. We may suggest that as copper was becoming an essential commodity in Mesopotamia the contacts with Oman became more regular and more formally organized, if not much more frequent, than they had been previously in order to safeguard the supplies. We must also remember that Dilmun was not the only source of copper available and transport down the Euphrates and the Tigris from the metalliferous zones of central and eastern Turkey was probably more cost effective than transport from Oman when the political situation in northern Syria allowed trading to take place.

The picture presented here of Arabia in the period from 5000 BC–3000 BC serves mainly to underline the paucity of the evidence. There was a small, permanent, indigenous population, with its own traditions and economy which were well adapted to the demands of a harsh environment. It seems likely that such settlements as existed were mostly small villages, perhaps inhabited on a seasonal basis and hard to locate in the archaeological record, lying in the oases or on major routes such as those to the copper resources of Oman. There is some evidence for a two-tier settlement pattern in the Ubaid period, with a few larger settlements which then disappear, only to re-emerge in the middle of the third millennium with the appearance of the tower houses of Oman and of an urban or semi-urban centre at Tarut. About the same time we have the first firm evidence for the resettlement of Bahrain. At no period were contacts with the wider world lost although their focus shifts; at the end of the fourth millennium the evidence comes largely from Oman, in the so-called Jemdat Nasr period, rather than from the Eastern Province which until this time seems to be the centre. It is only in the middle of the third millennium that the quality of our evidence improves to the point where we can begin to reconstruct something of the economy and society of the region with some confidence. In the next chapters we shall look at this evidence from the Eastern Province and Bahrain, and then at that from Oman.

Chapter 3

THE DEVELOPMENT OF DILMUN

The quality and quantity of the evidence for the development of Dilmun improves dramatically in the third millennium. In Mesopotamia textual references become more frequent and more comprehensible as the cuneiform script becomes more sophisticated. This allowed it to be used for longer, more informative inscriptions covering a much greater range of topics than the brief 'shorthand' notes of simple economic transactions which characterize the very earliest attempts at writing. There are, for example, a number of inscriptions belonging to some of the rulers of the early city states of Mesopotamia and their wives which refer to goods coming from Dilmun. Ur-Nanshe of Lagash, a contemporary of the people buried in the Royal tombs at Ur and so dating to about 2600 BC, mentions several times that he used wood from Dilmun for his extensive building programme, which included temples dedicated to some of the major gods of Sumer (Sollberger and Kupper 1971: 46).

Good building timber is not found in the northern Gulf itself so these texts strongly support the suggestion that Dilmun, whatever its precise location at this time, was still an important middleman, a role it had first played in the copper trade of the Uruk period. The timbers used by Ur-Nanshe may have originated in Oman, in south western Iran or in the Indus valley, an important source of hard woods in historical times. The wood may have been ferried to Dilmun by merchants from its country of origin, but then the inscriptions state specifically that it was brought to Lagash by the ships of Dilmun.

Snippets of information can also be gleaned from the many lists that seem to have been one of the passions of the Sumerian scribe. Lists of professions, for example, dating to the very beginning of the third millennium, include a Dilmun tax collector; lists of artefacts refer to a Dilmun axe, and several individuals have personal names which include the element Dilmun (Howard-Carter 1987). The references to Dilmun in the mythical texts date to the second, rather than the third millennium when few myths were written down. Although these myths probably preserve ancient oral traditions, they cannot be used uncritically as historical documents (see chapter 1).

The archaeological evidence also increases. Survey work has located a considerable number of sites of this period in Eastern Arabia (Fig. 3.1), although few have been excavated. (These surveys are published in *Atlal*, I, II and III.) Prior to the work of the international team carrying out these studies, Piesinger, working in the 1970s, surveyed from the Jabrin oasis in the south to Tarut island in the north and established

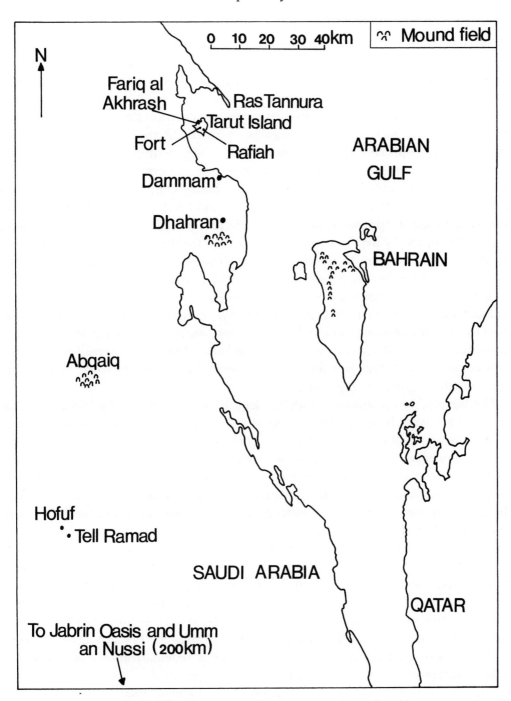

3.1 Third-millennium sites in the Eastern Province of Arabia.

the presence of third millennium pottery throughout the region, some of it apparently of Mesopotamian origin. This work formed the basis of her unpublished doctoral dissertation (Piesinger 1983). The results of these surveys also allow us to identify sites with different functions, we have fields of burial mounds and various settlements of different sizes and types. The settlements include what may, in spite of its small size, be the first urban centre in the Eastern Province. Its centre is located beneath the fort at Tarut and it can be suggested, for reasons which are discussed later in this volume, that it provided specialist goods and services to a large hinterland. The geographical location of the island strongly suggests that it was an important port on a coast which, it has already been noted, has few protected anchorages. Traditionally, the island has had two ports, one at Sanabis in the north-east and the other at Darin in the south. These anchorages are probably the reason for the presence of the early settlements here.

In addition, two 'village' sites were identified on the mainland and partly explored by Piesinger at Umm-an-Nussi and Umm-ar-Ramadh. The large numbers of burial mounds of third millennium date located at Abqaiq and Dhahran probably indicate the presence of other settlements in the Eastern Province which have yet to be identified, or which have been destroyed. Alternatively, it is possible that these mounds were used by nomadic groups as their tribal burial grounds. However, in the absence of evidence for partial and secondary burial, an indicator that bodies were being carried over considerable distances before burial, it seems more likely that the tumuli were built by settled groups living nearby.

The increase in the amount of archaeological evidence gives the impression that more people were living in the region overall, but this may well be an illusion. Prehistoric populations are notoriously difficult to calculate, even when far more detailed evidence is available than is the case with Arabia. As a general principle, adequate, reliable nutrition made possible by the advent of domestication, does tend to bring a natural, slow increase in population, which can be attributed more to a fall in the death rate than to a rise in the birthrate (Wrigley 1969). In Arabia the difficulty of calculating the size of the population is compounded by the presence of hunter-gatherers who seem to have been in the area since the late Holocene. Some of these nomadic groups may have begun to settle down by the early third millennium, either attracted by the better standard of living in the towns and villages or dispossessed by economic hardship. Modern ethnographic evidence indicates a natural tendency towards sedentarization in most nomadic groups (Cribb 1991: 39–43). As hunter-gatherers these groups are archaeologically almost invisible, but as villagers they may become visible in the archaeological record for the first time. Thus sedentarization can give a misleading impression of population increase.

There is no suggestion that the semi-nomadic or nomadic ways of life ceased with the establishment of agricultural communities. It is suggested that there would have been an ebb and flow between the two strategies. Causes of this movement probably included natural conditions such as variations in climate and rainfall causing wells to dry up, or the over-exploitation of game or other natural resources forcing changes in subsistence strategies. Changes in tribal territories as a result of warfare may also have occurred making certain areas inaccessible, so disrupting the annual migration cycle. Such a situation can be seen in recent times when friction between Iraq and Iran made many migration routes across the Zagros unusable, and a similar situation can be seen today on the borders of Afghanistan and the North-West frontier of Pakistan. Sometimes political circumstances may even have had the opposite effect, making it desirable for dissident groups to leave the settled life in favour of the safety of the desert. The need for maximum economic flexibility, to combat the marginal nature of the agricultural base over most of the Arabian peninsula and the frequently volatile nature of its politics, has always been a constant in the lives of the inhabitants of this area.

The apparent increase in population in Eastern Arabia in the third millennium, together with the presence of at least one more substantial settlement on Tarut island, also strongly suggests developments in social organization. The social structures appropriate to small isolated groups of people are inadequate to deal with larger groups and with the more complex economic and social relations for which we have evidence by the middle of the millennium.

These social structures can take several forms and it is arguable, on the basis of the archaeological remains, that two contrasting societies may have been emerging in the region, one in Eastern Arabia and Bahrain, the other further south in Oman and the Emirates. In the former area it will be suggested that we have at least one quasi-urban settlement at Tarut by the middle of the third millennium in addition to the villages identified above. The villages are sites composed of small rectangular structures, apparently domestic in character. No settlement sites of the period have been excavated in the area of the Dhahran or Abqaiq mound fields, although survey has identified a number of relevant occupation sites between al Khubar and Dammam, and there is another group around al Hasa (Potts *et al.* 1978: 9). There is also a small coastal settlement at the Qala'at al Bahrain by the middle of the third millennium. Oman and the Emirates present an obvious contrast, no clearly urban sites have been found, although Orchard and Stranger (1994) have recently challenged this view. Instead we have large fortified circular structures sometimes associated with other domestic buildings, of which the finest examples come from Hili in the Buraimi oasis and from Tell Abraq on the coast. These buildings lie in the oases west of the mountains and are often associated with copper sources in the hills nearby. An exception to this generalization can be seen at the site of Umm-an-Nar off the coast of Abu Dhabi, where only rectilinear buildings occur, but this seems to have been a special purpose site where goods were stored and then traded with Mesopotamia (Frifelt 1995 and chapter 6).

Contrasts are visible in burial customs too. In the mound fields of the Eastern

3.2 Umm-an-Nar type graves from Hamad Town and near Shakhura.

Province, and in Bahrain, the mounds seem normally to have housed one main burial, sometimes with a limited number of subsidiary ones. A certain amount of caution is necessary, however, in making this statement because an increasing number of burial rites are now known from Bahrain. For example, some graves which are close in plan to the Umm-an-Nar graves found typically further south, have now been excavated (Fig. 3.2), and these may well have contained multiple burials. They remain a minority. In the Eastern Province multiple burials are also known to occur. For example in the Dhahran mound field 120 burials were found in grave A6, while A5 had 52, but the excavators suggest that the tombs were often reused and it is no longer possible to tell how many of these bodies were deposited in the original grave (Zarins *et al.* 1984:

46). There is evidence that in the Dhahran field this reuse of the third millennium structures continued until the Hellenistic and Islamic periods; grave B17 was reused a number of times with an Islamic grave finally inserted on top of the capstone of the original burial (Frohlich 1985:10). In Bahrain, on the other hand, the majority of the multiple burials belong to the Kassite period and mounds do not seem to have been reutilised so extensively.

In the Oman peninsula, by contrast, burial for most of the third millennium is in large, complex, stone-built graves which can contain multiple burials of more than 150 people. These tombs frequently lie close to a tower house. The prevalence in Oman and the Emirates of multiple burials in a single tomb, often associated with large, circular, fort-like buildings of similar date, would seem to point to a different social structure to that in the Eastern Province and Bahrain, where we have seen that small group burials and rectangular houses are the norm. If it is accepted that burial rites and domestic housing in some way reflect the social structure of the societies in which they occur (e.g. Morris 1992 and Kent 1990), we may tentatively suggest that in Oman the large extended family, or clan, was the building block of society. To the north, tombs and houses only big enough for a single family may lead us to guess that the nuclear family was the basic unit here. The evidence, incomplete though it is, raises the possibility that the areas which interest us may have begun to develop in different directions and at different paces. The position of Umm-an-Nar at the junction of the two areas seems to show elements of both traditions. The magnificent multiple tombs, comparable to those in Oman, certainly point to the importance of the extended household, while the houses appear to be free-standing rectangular units, comparable to examples from Eastern Arabia. However, it is possible that these are special purpose storage units, rather than normal houses.

The archaeological evidence which will allow this tentative model of divergent social development to be evaluated now needs to be examined in more detail. We will look first at the evidence from Eastern Arabia and Bahrain dividing it into that from the first three-quarters of the third millennium and that from the 'classic' Early Dilmun period. Then, in later chapters, we will look at Umm-an-Nar and the Oman peninsula during the same period.

SETTLEMENT EVIDENCE FROM EASTERN ARABIA

The evidence for the early third millennium is still very sparse. No settlements were identified by Zarins and his team, but they may have been destroyed by wind erosion, or masked by the Islamic occupation mounds which now lie on the southern edge of the mound fields (Zarins *et al.* 1984: 26). The necessity of placing settlements within easy reach of the limited water supplies mean that the same locations are frequently reoccupied a number of times, while the habit, still seen today, of moving soil to create new date gardens further confuses the archaeological record. Smaller sites may have been totally destroyed by wind erosion or by agricultural activity. In her survey work Piesinger was able to report a number of badly deflated sites of the period in the Abqaiq area and at Umm-an-Nussi in the Jabrin oasis, in addition to the sites mentioned earlier in the Dammam area (Piesinger 1983: 490–6). Umm-an-Nussi is the most important of these and although small in area has a three-metre-high tell in its centre. It has traces of a regular street plan and of what may have been an enclosure wall around the site. The buildings seem to be rectangular domestic units and the pottery is said to include late Uruk, Jemdat Nasr and Hafit style wares. A macehead of Early Dynastic type is also reported, together with copper and stone artefacts (Piesinger 1983: 194), indicating usage from the middle of the fourth to the middle of the third millennia.

Preliminary exploration also took place at Umm-ar-Ramadh, which lies in the northwest of the al Hasa oasis on the shores of a fossil lake. Traces of structures could be seen on the surface over an area of several hundred metres and one building was excavated. It proved to be a rectangular 'house' composed of four small rooms parallel to each other, linked by a large room or courtyard to one side. No doors were recovered. The pottery is said to include chain-ridge ware like that from Bahrain, (see p. 53) and Mesopotamian Early Dynastic wares as well as Umm-an-Nar pottery from the Oman peninsula. This would indicate a date in the middle to late third millennium (Piesinger 1983: 206–9).

The most substantial evidence for the period comes from Tarut island, but only the most preliminary work could be undertaken because the oldest remains appear to lie in a small tell in the centre of the modern town, below the ruined fort. It is difficult even to assess the area of this tell, but it would not seem to exceed one hectare in area. A number of fine monumental stone blocks, probably the remains of buildings, and a large spring fed basin on the north-west edge of the tell have been reported (Piesinger 1983: 880). The fort was surveyed in a preliminary study by Bibby (1973) who claimed that four major phases could be identified below the fort, each associated with buildings. From the lowest level came some worked flint and what may be Ubaid pottery. Above this some Umm-an-Nar sherds were found (Fig. 3.3) together with chain-ridge ware identical with that found on Bahrain, as well as some slightly later Barbar ware (Potts 1990: 179). The finds suggest that the site may have been inhabited for well over a millennium. Bibby was unable to explore the rest of the modern settlement and it is possible that a lower town existed too. Worked blocks of masonry have been reported from a nearby drainage ditch.

Two other sites on the island have yielded finds dating from the middle of the third to the early second millennia; limited trenching at al-Rufayah south-east of the modern town was carried out by Dr A. Masry. This confirmed the presence of pottery dating from the middle of the third millennium (Masry 1974). Further small-scale work was carried out in the same area by Piesinger who found a number of unworked lumps of

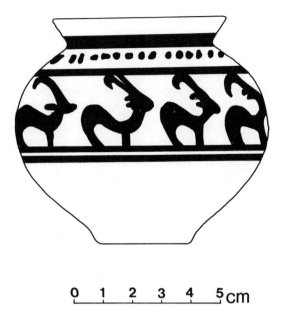

0 1 2 3 4 5 cm

3.3 Black on grey Umm-an-Nar pottery from Tarut.

lapis and copper in addition to pieces of worked, and partly worked steatite, throughout her excavation. Some of the sherds of steatite are decorated in the so-called
Intercultural style. A knobbed steatite lid, typical of City II levels on Bahrain was also
recovered (Piesinger 1983: 175–90). Pottery, and an almost complete steatite jar with
four vertically pierced lugs, probably of second millennium date, were found at
another site on the island, Fariq al-Akhrash (Bibby 1973: 37).

The sheer quantity of material, the presence of stone of central Arabian origin, and
the evidence of the unfinished pieces of steatite, which come mainly from al-Rufayah,
rather than from the fort, suggests that vessels of this material were being manufactured on Tarut island. They were certainly being finished and recut, and it is interesting that this is the only site so far where some of the vessels appear to have been
lathe turned. The possibility that vessels were being manufactured here has led to
much discussion especially as the iconography of these and other pieces from the island
published by Zarins (1978) belongs to the so-called Intercultural style first isolated by
Philip Kohl in his doctoral thesis (Kohl 1974). Pieces decorated in the Intercultural style
are also found in middle third-millennium levels at sites stretching from Mari on the
middle Euphrates via many of the major cities of the Sumerian plain, to Susa and the
site of Tepe Yahya near Kermanshah in south-west Iran, where the vessels were also
being manufactured (Lamberg-Karlovsky 1970). Many of the motifs on these highly
decorative and sophisticated pieces do not seem to belong to the Sumerian repertoire
and are more at home in south and eastern Iran, or even further afield in Baluchistan

and Central Asia. They include, for example, a humped bull, which is unknown in Mesopotamia until the Agade period *c.* 2350 BC and a kilted human figure with a hooked nose often shown with snakes. Other pieces show buildings with a curious concave lintel over the doors and walls apparently made of *barasti* or other light material which have no parallels in Mesopotamia either. They seem to be part of what Amiet has called the 'trans-Elamite culture' (Amiet 1986: 213), which is found from Susa in a great arc across south-west Iran and northwards through Seistan and into Central Asia. Influences from Baluchistan and the Indus valley can also be seen.

A study of the trace elements in the stone from which these vessels are made indicates that the raw material came from several different sources, all of them outside the Sumerian plain. At least two of them probably lie in Arabia, while the others were in Iran, notably in the area around the manufacturing centre at Tepe Yahya (Kohl, Harbottle and Sayre 1979). Kohl has also noted some correlation between material and design. The Intercultural style vessels tend to be in dark stone, while another group decorated with the dot and circle motif are normally made in a light grey softstone. This suggests a change in the source of supply of both raw materials and finished products some time in the last quarter of the third millennium when the dot and circle vessels begin to appear in quantity and the figurative vessels decline (Kohl 1986: 373). The softstone used to make pots at Tarut seems to have come from several of the sources identified, including the Yahya area in Iran. The later workshop at Failaka also re-used material from a variety of sources. It should be noted that the analyses undertaken by Kohl and his colleagues did not include any of the vessels made at Maysar in Oman as this material was not available to them. This new manufacturing centre may suggest a third Arabian source and makes the picture even more complex (Weisgerber 1981).

The similarity in the designs on pots from Yahya, Tarut and Failaka and the use of some stone from a common source raises a number of very interesting questions:
- why did craftsmen working in the Tarut area use stones and iconography apparently more at home in Iran?
- who were these craftsmen?
- were they natives of Tarut or were they, perhaps, emigrants from the south-west of Iran?
- if they were immigrants, did they then pass their skills on to local craftsmen who used stone from a variety of sources, including those nearest to them in Arabia ?
- how were the vessels manufactured in Tarut distributed to places like Adab on the Sumerian plain and Mari on the middle Euphrates ?

There can be no doubt that there were contacts between Tarut and south-west Iran, the iconographic parallels are too close and too numerous to be put down to chance. In addition to the steatite, some pieces of incised grey pottery decorated with designs identical to those on the Intercultural pots have been identified from the island and their closest parallels come from the site of Bampur in southern Iran (Zarins 1978 nos.

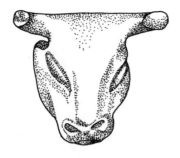

3.4 Copper bull's head from the Eastern Province.

198 and 201). On the mainland, black on red goblets from the Dhahran survey are also at home in Iran, as is some of the slightly later black on grey ware (Zarins *et al.* 1984: 32). Perhaps travelling craftsmen settled in Tarut because it was more conveniently located than their home base for forwarding goods to southern Mesopotamia? Perhaps unsettled conditions in Iran forced them to look for another home? A layer of charcoal overlies level IVB at Tepe Yahya, suggesting a destruction at the end of the period with the best evidence for the manufacturing of steatite vessels at the site (Lamberg-Karlovsky 1970: 85). Did craftsmen leaving Yahya bring half-finished pots with them to Tarut and pass on their skills? The redating of Yahya IVb 4–1 (Potts T. 1994: 260–1) makes this suggestion less attractive as the levels containing evidence for the manufacture of steatite vessels are now thought to date to the end of the third millennium and so could be later than the steatite-rich levels at Tarut. The Failaka material appears to be re-used and to date to the early second millennium, but it is not known how it reached the island or where it originated.

Other finds, too, point to Tarut's far-reaching network of contacts. A fine copper bull's head has recently been published by D.T. Potts from the island (Fig. 3.4), but its exact provenience and its present whereabouts are sadly unknown (Potts 1989: 25–6 Fig. 21). Potts points to a number of close parallels from Mesopotamia, including similar heads from Khafaje and Tell Agrab. The size of Potts' bull's head, estimated at about 4 cm, suggests it may have come originally from a piece of furniture or a musical instrument. Contacts with Mesopotamia are also indicated by jars of buff ware (Potts 1990: 181) and by various stone artefacts including a curious inlay of lapis lazuli showing a bearded figure with crimped wiglike hair and a cloak. This figure is also generally accepted as showing close affinities with pieces from Mesopotamia. Worked

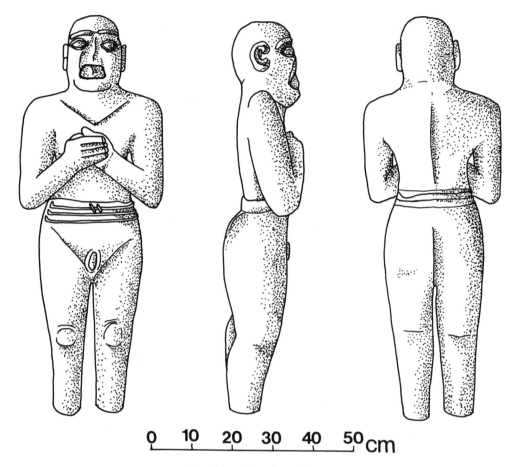

3.5 Male statue from Tarut.

and unworked lapis lazuli, from distant Badakhshan or Baluchistan, has also been found in the gardens at al Rufayah. Lapis seems to have travelled to Mesopotamia from the two known source areas, the more important in Badakhshan, and a second recently identified in Baluchistan, overland through Eastern Iran or across the Indian Ocean and up the Gulf from Harappan ports like Lothal (Potts T. 1994). Ports such as Tarut which lay on this route could have creamed off supplies for their own use, feeding their products, such as the softstone vessels, into the trade network in exchange.

The damaged stone statue of a standing nude male with clasped hands (Fig. 3.5) found in the gardens on Tarut provides further evidence for overseas connections. He has often been compared to votive statues from Sumer, dating to the middle of the third millennium. The clasped hands and the triple belt, which is his sole adornment, are features which can be exactly paralleled in the Early Dynastic repertoire, but the low forehead and the shell-like treatment of the ears also suggest comparisons with the

0 1 2 3 4 5 cm

3.6 Black on red jar from Tarut.

very limited amount of Harappan sculpture known to us. The well-known figure of a priest/king from Mohenjo-Daro has the same features, as too does a head from Susa which Amiet identifies as an import from the Indus valley (Amiet 1986: 144, 148, Fig. 95). The forehead and the ears on the two are certainly very similar. If the Tarut piece can be shown to combine elements from both the Indus valley and Sumerian traditions, perhaps it should be seen as the product of a local workshop on Tarut itself? The softstone vessels certainly indicate the presence of a stone-working tradition.

Further fragments of copper and some fine pieces of black on red (Fig. 3.6) and black on grey painted Umm-an-Nar pottery demonstrate contacts with Oman, in the opposite direction. Some of the less elaborate, and slightly later, softstone vessels from Tarut decorated with the dot and circle motif find their closest parallels in examples from Maysar. It seems likely that Tepe Yahya was no longer in use as a production centre by the second millennium and that the main production centres were centred in Oman.

The presence of these later styles suggests that the Tarut settlement continued into this period, but it is not clear whether the production of vessels also continued.

A number of badly damaged cist graves were found on Tarut island and a large collection of artefacts was retrieved. Most of them had been obtained by local residents from gardeners working in the gardens. Metalwork is reported, but no details are available. However, even without details of these finds, the presence of the range of highly sophisticated artefacts and exotic raw materials already described demonstrates wide-ranging foreign connections and the presence of skilled craftsmen able to work in stone and metal. This gives weight to the suggestion that, in spite of the small area of the tell site, by the middle of the third millennium, the island of Tarut housed a genuinely urban centre, which boasted a number of specialist craftsmen and was involved in a trading network with other centres in Iran, the Indus valley and southern Mesopotamia. The presence of such a diverse and skilled group of people and the evidence for a complex trading network both strongly suggest the presence of some sort of central administration. Direct evidence for this is sadly lacking, unless we can, with extreme caution, suggest that the monumental masonry may be the remains of public buildings.

Graves

We will now look more closely at the finds from the mound fields south of Dhahran. The fields, when first reported, were said to contain thousands of graves, but only 900 survived when they were counted by archaeologists in the early 1980s, and most had been re-used in later times and so had been considerably disturbed. Some of the finds date to the Hellenistic period, when some graves were reused and more seem to have been added. However, a limited amount of pottery of early third millennium date has been identified, including one or two vessels which seem to have originated in Mesopotamia and what was originally said to be a Jemdat Nasr cylinder seal (Zarins *et al.* 1984: 37). It has now been shown to date to the later second millennium (Lombard 1988). Grave 2 yielded a so-called Persian Gulf seal, probably of late third millennium date, while a Mesopotamian duck weight from this grave belongs to the same period (Piesinger 1983: 104 and Fig. 186, 7 and 11).

There are also a few pieces of so-called Umm-an-Nar ware from the mound fields. This pottery is also of third-millennium date, it was first identified further south and is now known to occur on Tarut as well. The most characteristic vessels of this ware are simple jars of red or grey wares, decorated with geometric patterns in black paint. Naturalistic motifs representing cervids or caprids, for example, are also known. The pottery is closely linked to similar black on grey wares from Iran and is generally thought to date to the first three quarters of the third millennium. Goblets, some of which have parallels in Baluchistan and the Indus also occur (Zarins *et al.* 1984: 32).

Structurally the Dhahran graves are similar to ones thought to be of comparable date on Bahrain, in the Medinat Hamad field for example, where Umm-an-Nar pottery also occurs. These graves have a central chamber, usually above ground, but sometimes sunk into the rock, closed with a capstone and surrounded by a ring wall. The whole construction was then covered with a mound of stones and earth (Zarins *et al.* 1984: 28). Variations in the size and shape of the central chamber are found and there is a small group of poorly built cist graves, dating to the same period. The excavators see a rapid expansion of the Dhahran field *c.* 2500 BC. The position in the Abqaiq field seems to be similar, although some of the graves there may go back slightly earlier (Zarins 1989: 74). Another large concentration of tumuli was explored here and Piesinger reported Mesopotamian brown wares of Early Dynastic, middle of the third millennium, date in ten of the fourteen tumuli excavated. Umm-an-Nar wares occur with the Mesopotamian material and a few exotic beads of lapis and carnelian were also recovered (Piesinger 1983: 118).

BAHRAIN: THE SETTLEMENT EVIDENCE

Later third-millennium settlement occurs on the main Bahrain island, where, as we have already seen, the earliest settlement dates to the Ubaid period. The island's fresh water springs and fertile northern shore made it an attractive prospect in comparison with the inhospitable coast of much of the Eastern Province and it is rather surprising that there is, at present, virtually no evidence that the island was inhabited in the fourth millennium. One sherd of polychrome Jemdat Nasr ware is recorded from the site of the Barbar temple (Mortensen 1970: 390) and there are two jars on display in the National Museum which, judging from their shape, may also date to this period, although all traces of paint have been lost (Vine 1993). A round stamp seal from al Hajjar, published by Michael Rice (Rice 1988: pl. III, 1972) is also said to be Jemdat Nasr in style, but may have been recut, which together with the 'heirloom factor', make it a poor dating criterion. It may have been deposited in the grave long after it was first made.

When we reach the middle of the third millennium the evidence for settlement is a little more plentiful, although sites are still scarce. Survey work has improved the picture and Larsen (1983b: 78) lists seven sites which have yielded pottery of the so-called City I period. The most important excavations have taken place at the Bahrain fort, or Qala'at (Fig. 3.7), while the site at Diraz may also date back to the same time, while recent work at Saar has added another site of this date to Larsen's tally (Woodburn and Crawford 1994: 92). Work over the past ten years means that there is now little doubt that by the middle of the third millennium Bahrain boasted a flourishing local economy based on fishing and agriculture as well as a burgeoning network of overseas contacts. The evidence for settlement is still slight, and still comes mainly

3.7 Qalaʿat al Bahrain, aerial view.

from the work of the Danish expedition at the Qalaʿat. Here period Ia probably dates to the middle of the third millennium, Ib to the later Agade period and period IIa/c, the Early Dilmun or Barbar II period, to the Ur III to Old Babylonian periods. The earliest levels of the nearby Barbar temple may also date back to period Ib, although Højlund considers them to belong to period IIa (Højlund and Andersen 1994: chart 141).

The Qalaʿat lies on the fertile north coast of the island about four kilometres west of the modern capital of Manama and covers an area 300 x 600 m. The old coastline has been fundamentally altered by land reclamation, but the site boasted a good harbour prior to this. The Qalaʿat forms perhaps the largest tell site in the Gulf and is topped by the remains of a fine Portuguese fort. Almost every period of the island's history from *c.* 2,500 BC to the sixteenth century AD is represented. The earliest remains found by the Danish expedition at the base of their trenches consisted of pottery and occupation debris embedded in *farush*, a limestone conglomerate formed by standing water, and in the clean sand below it. Below this sand is the sterile green clay which marked the ancient ground surface. No structural remains were found associated with these earliest artefacts so they may represent the rubbish thrown out of the nearby settle-

3.8 Chain-ridge ware from Saar.

ment, rather than the remains of the settlement itself. This phase has been attributed by Højlund to period Ia (Højlund and Andersen 1994: 68).[8]

Above the *farush* stone, walls were found which are too fragmentary to form a coherent plan, but which are oriented north–south and run under the later fortification wall of period II (Højlund and Andersen 1994: plan 1). Open spaces, rooms and three wells were identified. North of the City Wall another heavy wall of Ib date was identified over a short stretch and it is suggested that this may be a forerunner of the later wall (Højlund and Andersen 1994: 68). The levels attributed to this phase were given the grandiose designation of City 1, but it seems from the evidence that we may be looking at something closer to a fishermen's village (Bibby 1986: 114). The pottery from both periods Ia and Ib includes a majority of sherds of Højlund's ware type 1 with exploding grits which dominates the local pottery repertoire. Pottery decorated with chain-ridges is found in these levels (Fig. 3.8) and is now regarded as the hallmark of this period (Højlund and Andersen 1994: chapter 5). Chain-ridge ware is seldom found in the grave mounds and, until recently, this pottery was not known from any other

---

[8] Bibby attributes levels 22–8 to City 1 and levels 29–31 to the pre-City one phase. Larsen, however, regards level 26 as the first City I level (Larsen 1983a). Højlund also considers that City II starts in level 26 and continues to level 22.

stratified contexts on the island. It has now been identified from the blown sand at the base of a five-metre-deep sounding below the early second-millennium temple at the site of Saar (Woodburn and Crawford 1994). It is not yet clear whether these sherds relate to the earliest permanent occupation of the site or pre-date it. Chain-ridge ware also occurs in the Eastern Province as we saw at Tarut. A small proportion of the sherds from the earliest levels at the Qala'at are of foreign origin. Ten per cent of the pottery is said to be in the Mesopotamian tradition and 3 per cent in that of Umm-an-Nar, originating in the Oman peninsula. One important Mesopotamian sherd from period Ib, originally published by Laessoe in 1957, has a cuneiform inscription of quantity on it indicating a capacity of 167 *sila* and has close parallels at Nippur in the Ur III period (Højlund and Andersen 1994: 168).

A copper spearhead and other artefacts, together with scraps of copper, were found in some quantity in both periods Ia and Ib (City 1) levels suggesting contacts with Oman. Copper seems to have been worked at the Qala'at as crucible and mould fragments were also found, though there is no evidence for smelting. The metal seems to have been traded as ingots (Højlund and Andersen 1994: 73–178). A single, moulded clay figurine of a naked woman from one of the later period 1b levels, in Bibby's north wall excavation, is Mesopotamian in origin. This figure is probably out of context as stylistically it would appear to belong to the Old Babylonian period *c.* 1800 BC. Another find which is probably also intrusive is a weight of Indus valley type attributed by Bibby to this phase (Bibby 1984: 110), but convincingly re-attributed to period IIa by Højlund. The only evidence for contacts with the Indus valley in period Ib comes from a small number of sherds in what Højlund has called the Eastern Tradition.

Absolute dates for period Ib and its predecessor are still unclear. The local pottery typical of the period does not occur in well-dated contexts outside Bahrain so that no firm dates can be derived by comparison. The chronology of the imported Umm-an-Nar pottery is still not clear either and it seems it may have been in use for most of the third millennium. The Mesopotamian pottery has its closest parallels in the late Agade and early Ur III periods according to Højlund's analysis (Højlund and Andersen 1994). The only artefact from period Ib which can be dated with any certainty is the Indus valley weight. This would also support a date towards the end of the third millennium, but it seems highly likely that it is intrusive in period Ib and belongs with other similar weights in level IIa. A date in the last quarter of the third millennium for period Ib seems preferable and the earliest Ia remains may be several hundred years older.

This dating would agree with the evidence from the succeeding period IIa for a date around 2000 BC for its lower levels. The C14 dates suggest a slightly earlier date (Højlund and Andersen 1994: 174). The tablet found outside the wall in the north-west sounding, and apparently dating to the post-Ur III period (Brunswig *et al.* 1983), cannot be used to substantiate the date proposed for IIa because its association with the wall is not stratigraphically demonstrated. It was, however, found in association with a Persian Gulf seal (see below) and thus serves as a guide to the date of that seal. Seals of this type are said to come from Ur III contexts at the site of Ur itself and one example, BM 122187, may date back to the Agade period. This would indicate that the seals first came into circulation in that period, rather earlier than is generally thought. However, seals are very easily displaced in the archaeological record and their archaeological contexts are rather poor (Mitchell 1986: 279–80).

In summary, the evidence from the excavations of the so-called City 1 at the Qala'at indicates that there was a small settlement here from the middle of the third millennium, possibly walled, which was in contact with Mesopotamia, Oman and areas to the east. The finds of copper ingots suggest that the contacts with Mesopotamia may already have been linked to the copper trade, although the textual evidence from Ur III Mesopotamia during the Ur III period indicates that trade was centred on Magan/Oman until the end of the third millennium. There is no evidence for large-scale commercial operations in Bahrain at this stage.

Graves

Bahrain has been famous for its vast mound fields of ancient burial mounds since travellers like Captain Durand and the Bents reported in the last quarter of the nineteenth century on features of interest which the island offered (Rice 1984). The enormous numbers of tumuli on Bahrain noted by these early visitors, the apparent absence of settlements and the presence of the magical sweet water springs which well up under the sea as well as on land, led many early scholars to suggest that the island was a sacred island of the dead. It is now clear that the burial mounds were in use for much longer than originally believed and were still being constructed in the first centuries of the Christian era so that fewer of them than was originally thought belong to the Dilmun period. This observation and the increase in the number of settlement sites now being identified suggests that the mounds represent the burial places of the island's own inhabitants and not those of pious foreigners. The idea of Bahrain as a giant necropolis must be abandoned.

The mound fields lie mostly in the north of the island, although a field is marked on an older map at Mattala in the south-west of the island in what is now a restricted zone (Glob 1968), and a second lies half way down the west coast at Umm Jidr (Cleuziou 1981), close to the al Areen wildlife park. The mounds in the north lie mainly on rock outcrops so that valuable agricultural ground was not given over to the dead. In addition to the mound burials a number of subterranean burials have now been discovered in the course of construction work, most importantly at al Hajjar, also in the north of the island (Rice 1984).

It seems that the earliest mounds, such as many of the ones in the Hamad town group, date back to around 2500 BC, or a little earlier. The dating of burials is not an

3.9 'Grave pot' of red ware.

easy matter especially when, as in Bahrain, many of them have been robbed and re-used in antiquity. Because of this the contents may only reflect the latest date at which they were disturbed, rather than the period at which they were constructed. In addition, the goods buried in graves are not always the same as those used by the living so that pottery types, for example, may be specific to the graves and almost unknown from stratified occupation sites. The so-called grave pots of the early second millennium made of fine red ware, bag-shaped with a ridged neck, are a good example of this (Fig. 3.9). They are frequently found in burials, but occur very rarely in other contexts, which makes their dating very difficult.

There is also the problem caused by the deposition in graves of precious objects which were already ancient when the burial took place. An example of this problem can be seen in the splendid honeycomb grave complex at Saar (Fig. 3.10), which was mainly used in the early second millennium, but which contains a number of artefacts and seals which are of third-millennium date, such as a magnificent steatite Hut pot (Crawford and al Sindi 1996). Were these objects heirlooms or does the complex date back to the third millennium? At present it is not easy to answer this question. Finally, it must be remembered that observed differences in burial rites and in the construction of graves may not be due to chronological factors, but to social ones.

In spite of all these problems, there are some grave mounds on Bahrain which certainly date back to the middle to late third millennium and Ibrahim has suggested that

3.10 Grave complex at Saar.

the smaller, lower mounds which usually contain only a single primary burial in a stone chamber in the centre of a low ring wall should be regarded as the earliest in the sequence (Ibrahim 1982). Lowe also adds that these graves seldom have a capstone and that secondary burials are unusual (Lowe 1986: 74). Some of these graves have yielded black on red Umm-an-Nar type pottery from Oman, and none has yet been found to contain the ridged ware typical of the early second millennium on the island. The Umm-an-Nar style pottery links these graves with the mainland and also with eastern Iran.

Other types of burial mound also belong to the third millennium. They consist of a small group of largely unpublished examples which are very similar in plan to examples found on the island of Umm-an-Nar and in the oases of Oman and the Emirates. A photograph of one fine example can be seen on the wall of the National

Museum in Manama and is also illustrated in Vine 1993: 34 (see also Fig. 3.2). The resemblance should not be over-emphasized as there are also significant differences. Where the Umm-an-Nar examples have the outer circular wall faced with fine stone blocks precisely tailored to fit together, the Bahrain ones do not. This may be explained by the absence of suitable stone on the island. The Bahrain ones stand on a plinth of small stones, in some cases heavily plastered, as do some of the Umm-an-Nar examples, but there the plinths are built of well-cut stone. The internal organization of the graves is, on the other hand, very similar to that found in the graves on Umm-an-Nar island with a variable number of compartments being formed by partition walls, often divided by a central passage. The Kassite pottery found in some of these graves on Bahrain is probably due to secondary usage at a later date.

SUMMARY

The evidence is still insufficient to allow us to paint a detailed picture of the people living in the Eastern Province of Arabia and on the island of Bahrain in the first half of the third millennium. No houses of this period have been excavated, but it seems that there was a settled population of agriculturalists and fishermen living in villages and small towns along the coast. We know virtually nothing of the agricultural base, although the main categories of livestock had been domesticated since the fourth millennium. It seems possible that the camel was domesticated on the Arabian mainland before the end of the third millennium, but the evidence is still flimsy. The people were engaged in commercial activities which brought them into contact with Mesopotamia, Iran, Oman and the Indus valley. We can suggest that they were already involved in transporting goods to Mesopotamia, although Oman was the main focus of the copper trade at this time.

The only evidence for sophisticated craft production comes from Tarut in the Eastern Province, probably the only urban centre in the Gulf region, where high quality stone-working was undertaken. Period I levels at the Bahrain Qalaʿat which, on present evidence, was a mere village, have produced evidence for simple metalworking using open moulds for casting. Højlund has suggested that pottery-making at the same site was still at a household level as all the decorated wares seem to be imported and there is little evidence for anything except cooking pots being produced at the site.

Burial was generally in tumuli containing a single body and there is little evidence of a stratified society in what survives of the grave goods. The presence of a few graves related to those of the Umm-an-Nar culture raise the possibility of the presence of people from other parts of the Gulf also resident on Bahrain itself. We can speculate, by analogy with today, that there was probably also a mobile, nomadic or semi-nomadic population in the Eastern Province at least, which is archaeologically invisible, but which may have played an important part in transmitting goods and ideas from one part of the Gulf to another.

The agricultural, economic and cultural foundations existed to allow the remarkable expansion which marked the end of the third and the beginning of the second millennia, the period of Dilmun's greatest prosperity and influence.

Chapter 4

THE EXPANSION OF DILMUN: SETTLEMENT AND ARCHITECTURE

The dramatic expansion of settlement on Bahrain (Fig. 4.1) and the accompanying evidence for greatly increased prosperity in the so-called Early Dilmun period, belongs to the first quarter of the second millennium. This is the time when the focus of settlement seems to shift from Arabia to Bahrain. No new sites are reported from the Eastern Province, but Larsen reports that the number of sites on the islands more than doubles from seven to sixteen (Larsen 1983b: 78). Others have identified more sites since Larsen's survey was completed making the expansion even more marked. Larsen calls this period the Barbar II phase, while Højlund prefers the term Early Dilmun period. This expansion of settlement can be correlated with the moment when the Oman

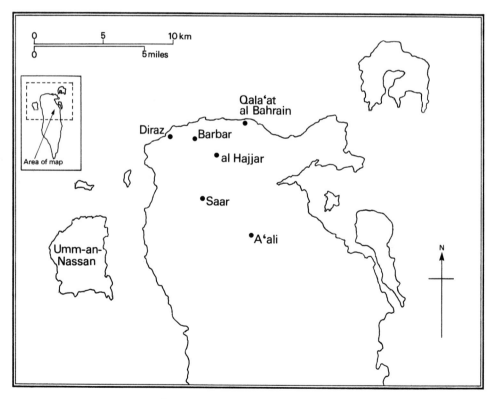

4.1 Map showing some of the main sites on Bahrain.

peninsula saw a marked change in settlement pattern and many of the tower houses were abandoned (see chapter 6). The texts from Mesopotamia confirm a change in the trading patterns at the end of the Ur III period and tell us that international commerce became centred on Dilmun instead of Magan. The economic centre of gravity seems to have shifted northwards with major consequences for the prosperity of both the areas concerned.

As in the pre-Dilmun or Barbar I period described in the last chapter, the subsistence economy of Bahrain seems to have been a mixed one with agriculture and fishing playing important roles. Work at the Qalaʿat al Bahrain and at Saar, a large village or small town in the north-west of the island, allows us to begin to reconstruct the subsistence base of the period. The animal bones show that cattle, pig, sheep, and goat were all present as domesticates. A few donkey bones were identified from the Qalaʿat, but it was not possible to tell if they were domesticated. It is interesting that no camel bones have yet been found at this site, although a very small number are found at Saar. It is suggested that both the sheep at the Qalaʿat, which are larger than the native Gulf breeds, and those from Saar which show a wide range of physical characteristics, may have been imported to the island. The pigs, which do not occur naturally in the area, must also have been brought in. The cattle were apparently used for traction as well as for meat. Dog was also present and, rather surprisingly, the remains show cut marks which indicate they may have been eaten (Uerpmann in Højlund and Andersen 1994: 417–54; Dobney and Jacques 1994).

A limited range of wild animal remains was also present and includes the remains of mongoose, possibly imported from the Indian subcontinent, hare, fox, oryx and gazelle (Fig. 4.2). The latter were probably hunted for meat, but did not form a significant element of the diet at either site. Cat was also found, but it is not clear whether it was domesticated. These remains suggest that the land environment on the island of Bahrain was similar to that of today. The sea also played a vital role in feeding the population as it still does today. Fishing for food was of much greater importance to the people who lived at the Qalaʿat and at Saar than either hunted or domesticated animals. It is estimated that 60 per cent by weight of the bones at the Qalaʿat were of fish which must have provided most of the protein in the local diet. An even higher percentage was found at Saar. In addition to the fish and sea mammals, such as dugong and tortoise for which there is also evidence, shells of oysters and other bivalves are everywhere. Some may have been used as bait, and some may be the result of pearl fishing, but many seem to have been eaten, as they are often found dumped in very large numbers around cooking areas in the houses at Saar.

The range of fish species found strongly suggests that a number of different fishing techniques were being used. There is archaeological evidence for the use of copper fish-hooks and in addition it seems highly probable that fixed nets were also employed as they are today. Although there is no direct evidence for boats from Saar, part of a model

4.2 Drawing of gazelle, and a Dilmun seal showing two gazelle.

boat was found in City II levels at the Qala'at (Højlund and Andersen 1994: 471), while small sailing boats are shown on the contemporary seals, some apparently made of reeds or palm stems. Recent finds of large pieces of bitumen, used to caulk vessels, found at Ras al Junayz have the impressions of wooden planks visible on their surfaces. This is allowing scholars to reconstruct the shape of the boats from which they came (Cleuziou 1996). The texts from Mesopotamia refer specifically to boats from Dilmun. This confirms that ocean-going boats were available, so deep sea fishing was also possible.

The remains of plants do not survive well from these sites and in spite of an extensive flotation programme at Saar (Nesbitt 1993) much of the information comes from impressions and the remains of the chaff used to temper pottery or to mix bitumen to the desired consistency. Date stones are the only botanical remains to be found in quantity and dates were obviously an important element in the diet. This is borne out by various studies of the teeth from contemporary burials which are notable for the large numbers of holes, probably caused by too many sweet things in the diet (Frohlich 1986). Apart from this, cereals such as six-row barley and a naked hulled wheat are known (Willcox in Højlund and Andersen 1994). A single flax seed comes from below the first building in the test pit in the temple at Saar, but the context is not secure (de Moulins in Crawford *et al.* 1997: 79). Rather surprisingly, no sorghum or sisyphus seeds have been recovered from either site. Charcoal remains show that acacia and tamarisk wood was being used in addition to that from the ubiquitous date palm. From Saar comes evidence for what is probably a non-native mangrove as well, archaeological confirmation perhaps of the timber trade mentioned in the texts (Gale 1994).

The limited evidence for cereals is sufficient to suggest that simple irrigation techniques may have been in use on the island as their cultivation would not have been possible without it. Dates could not have been grown in quantity without irrigation either and the presence of both date wood and date fibres woven into baskets and mats is good evidence that there was a plentiful local supply. The alternative is that the cereals were imports, but Potts has recently put forward convincing arguments against this (Potts 1993a *contra* Edens 1992). Recent finds by a Japanese team at Umm-es-Sejour, until recently one of the biggest springs on the island, may provide us with evidence for such an irrigation system. A number of channels leading from two fine stone-built wells have been uncovered (Fig. 4.3) (Konishi 1994). Similar channels were identified running from the base of the so-called sacred well at the Barbar temple and both systems can tentatively be seen as the head of some sort of irrigation network. The full publication of the results of the work of the Japanese is awaited with much interest.

SETTLEMENT

There is little evidence for settlement from Eastern Arabia in the Early Dilmun period, although survey identified a number of sites of this date between al Khubar and

4.3 Umm-es-Sejour, aerial view.

4.4 Barbar ware, a ridged storage jar.

Dammam (Potts *et al.* 1978: 9). In the Dhahran area the majority of the grave mounds probably date to this period, although many have since been re-used. More sherds of typical early second millennium Barbar pottery were found in the Abqaiq region (Piesinger 1978: 493, 502). Sherds of this distinctive pottery have been found over a much wider area which reaches as far as the Indian Ocean coast of the Oman peninsula at Khor Ile-sud (Edens 1994), and perhaps even further south (Fig. 4.4). The presence of the pottery cannot by itself be taken as evidence of Dilmun settlement, but does obviously suggest contact, whether direct or indirect.

Bahrain, however, is more informative and has provided us with limited information on town planning, monumental buildings and domestic structures all of which illustrate the increase in social complexity which characterizes this period. We will look first at the remains from the Qalaʿat al Bahrain which is considered a fully urban site by this period when almost forty-two hectares of land were enclosed within the fortification wall which is the outstanding feature of this period (Larsen 1983b: 47). The massive city wall has been traced round most of the Qalaʿat. It was best preserved on the southern part of the tell where Bibby describes how it still stood eight feet high with a plastered outer face and was topped with a walkway which was protected with another thinner wall, four feet high, on its outer edge to shelter patrolling sentries (Bibby 1972: 359). This description should be treated with some caution as the more fully excavated wall on the north-east of the site was built in two successive phases, the second dating to the post-Dilmun occupation of the area and some of the more elaborate features in the south wall sounding may also relate to the post-Dilmun period. Bibby also reports a square tower strengthening the wall to the south-west. Whatever the details of its construction in its first phase, the wall represented a formidable barrier to raiders and suggests the wealth of the town inside of which, sadly, few traces remain. The Early Dilmun date of the first major city wall is suggested by the find of a cuneiform tablet lying about seven metres outside it, on the beach, and dated to *c.* 1950 BC on the basis of its style. Unfortunately no direct stratigraphic connection exists between the tablet and the wall (Brunswig *et al.* 1983: 107).

Inside the wall, buildings were only found to the north, on the seaward side of the tell. There is obvious continuity with the stone walls dating back to period Ib, which were used as footings for new ones. Some of the walls were cleared away to make a passage parallel with the inner face of the city wall. The materials and building technique are also closely similar. Bibby's claim that his City I ended with a disastrous fire must now be discounted. The ash layer on which he based his interpretation has now been shown to be related to a group of ovens close to the city wall. There is no general evidence for a fire (Højlund and Andersen 1994: 470). Remains of two streets running at right angles to the wall and parallel to each other suggest a regular layout of streets, something which can be seen more clearly at Saar (see p. 67). Each street gives access to a well, and in addition, the more easterly leads to a postern gate in the wall. No complete house plans were recovered, although a number of rectangular rooms can be identified (Fig. 4.5). The area was badly damaged by a moat, apparently contemporary with the Islamic fort, which cut through the area under excavation. A group of weights and seals were recovered in period IIa, several from two rooms in a building immediately south-east of the gate which led Bibby to interpret these as part of a customs house where goods coming into the town were taxed (Bibby 1972: 372). This explanation now

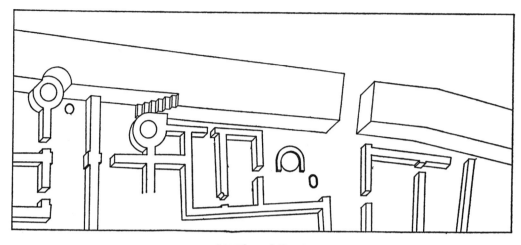

4.5   Plan of City 2.

looks untenable as seals and weights have been found widely distributed in ordinary domestic contexts at Saar and cannot be taken to indicate any special status for the buildings in which they are found. Finally, in the central area of the site, it seems that a re-evaluation of the plans and sections of the old excavations suggests the presence, in the area later occupied by the Assyrian Palace, of one or more building complexes which may have been warehouses (*Society for Arabian Studies Newsletter* 1995.6:10). If this should prove to be the case we have the first evidence for some kind of central authority, probably with redistributive functions.

The shore area was rebuilt twice in periods IIb and c on fundamentally the same lines. Modifications can be seen in IIc when the passage parallel with the wall is blocked off and one of the wells (19) is also found in a walled area, rather than in a public street. Behind this well is a flight of steps apparently leading up onto the wall. At some point an additional curtain wall was built in front of the old one to strengthen it. The end of period IIc should probably be placed in the eighteenth century BC and this area then seems to have been uninhabited for a time, although other parts of the site continue in use. After a time the second town wall was built partly on top of the original one, as we mentioned above.

The best information on the layout of settlements and on domestic architecture comes from the site of Saar on Bahrain, about seven kilometres south-west of the Qala'at, where work has been in progress since 1990 under the auspices of the London–Bahrain Archaeological Expedition (Fig. 4.6).[9] The site lies below the eastern arc of the Saar ridge on which lay one of the most extensive mound fields on the island.

---

[9] See Crawford 1993; Killick *et al.* 1991; Moon *et al.* 1995; Killick 1997; and Woodburn and Crawford 1994 for preliminary reports on the excavations at Saar.

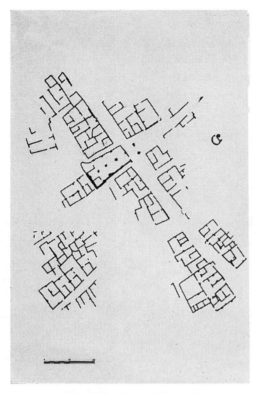

4.6 Plan of the large village of Saar.

(The mound field has now been largely cleared for development.) The ground slopes gently down towards the modern date gardens to the east where there is ample water and some fertile land for gardens. A stone-lined well, cut deep into the virgin rock, has been found in this area and may have been in use throughout the life of the settlement. It seems probable that the sea came up almost to the foot of the settlement in the late third and early second millennia and that boats could be beached here in safety. The ridge provided shelter from the prevailing winds and it would appear that the site was carefully chosen to provide the essentials of water and shelter without impinging on scarce supplies of agricultural land. It is difficult to estimate the total area of the site as the perimeter has yet to be finally determined, but it probably covered about 2.5 ha.

The street plan is remarkably regular with two main roads which meet in a T-junction in front of the temple which crowns the highest point on the site. One road runs approximately north–south, parallel to the coast, while the other runs east down the slope towards the suggested site of the harbour, the gardens and the well. A third wide road runs parallel to the northern sector of the first and further to the west behind the temple. Smaller side roads intersect the large roads at irregular intervals

4.7 A typical house at Saar.

forming what is almost a grid plan and dividing the buildings into blocks of four or five houses. The ordered look to the settlement is reinforced by the extraordinary regularity of the terraces of stone houses many of which are built to the same basic plan (Fig. 4.7). This consists of a rectangular building with a small covered room in one corner and an L-shaped outer area. Some also had an open yard at the rear. The L-shaped area housed water basins (Fig. 4.8), ovens (Fig. 4.9) and pits in some of which large jars were stored. Other pits were carefully plastered, but their function is unknown, perhaps they were for water storage. It seems likely that this outer area was covered with a light roof of palm leaves, in contrast to the wood and plaster roof of which traces have been found in the inner room. This standard house plan was frequently modified through time and a striking example of this can be seen in House 53 which is built over and incorporates some features of earlier buildings. In its final form it is one of the latest buildings on the site and instead of being part of a terrace, is a free-standing 'villa' with workshops and courtyards (Moon and Killick 1995). On the other hand, many of the minor modifications which can be seen in the life of particular 'standard' houses can probably be related to changes in the social structure of the group living in them. For example, when a child married a door might be broken through into the neighbouring house to provide more space, or when an elderly rela-

4.8 A double basin from House 100 at Saar.

tive died a group of rooms might be sold off as an independent dwelling. In this way the original plan of the building is modified through time although its original structure is still discernable.

Another anomalous area lies in the north-west of the site. These structures are small and rather ramshackle with large numbers of cooking and storage installations, and seem to have developed in a haphazard way. These rooms belong to a late phase of the settlement and seem to represent a period when the planning controls, which are indicated by the standardized nature of the earlier houses and the regularity of the layout, were no longer enforced. If such regulations did exist, we are bound to deduce the presence of a strong central authority somewhere on the island, if not at Saar itself where there is, as yet, no evidence for administrative buildings.

An area of what is probably contemporary housing was partially explored at the site of Diraz, between Saar and the Qala'at, but the published information is only sufficient to be able to say that the buildings do not seem to conform to the same plan as those at Saar. At least one appears to consist of a number of small rooms round a courtyard, but may have been part of a terrace (al Tikriti 1975: 18). At the moment there are no parallels and no antecedents for the Saar housing on Bahrain itself, but it is difficult to believe that this highly organized community was a first attempt at 'town planning'.

4.9 Tannur and fireplace from House 203 at Saar.

The antecedents of the Standard house plan at Saar remain unknown. It is possible that the houses from City 1 levels at the Qalaʿat might prove to conform to this plan if complete examples are ever retrieved and some unpublished houses from the site of al Hajjar would appear to be similar. Some of the broadly contemporary houses at Maysar in Oman appear to be laid out to the same plan and further details on this site are awaited with great interest.[10]

Some time during City II a new Early Dilmun settlement was founded on the low-lying island of Failaka, off the coast of Kuwait. The island lies in the mouth of the bay of Kuwait and has obvious strategic importance for ships heading for the mouth of the Shatt al Arab. The material culture of the new settlement is identical with that on Bahrain itself and is usually interpreted as some kind of trading colony established by Dilmun at the height of its prosperity. The settlement on Failaka is on several Tells in the south-west of the island, and remains dating to the Early Dilmun period have been found on three of them. The earliest are on the north part of Tell F3 and consist of a number of rectangular, stone built rooms on either side of a street which resemble the remains from the Qalaʿat. It is not clear if these rooms belong to one large complex or

---

[10] No Barbar pottery has been reported from this site and its date relative to Saar is not entirely clear.

to a terrace of smaller ones (Højlund 1987: Fig. 613, houses 26–29 and ?31.) A fine kiln was also uncovered to the south. Tell F6 revealed the remains of a possible temple which is described below, while the third Tell, G3, revealed only a few remains which included some evidence for metal-working (Calvet and Gachet 1990; Calvet and Salles 1986; Salles 1984).

TEMPLES

Returning to the main Bahrain island, no monumental buildings, other than the city wall, were recovered at the Qala'at, but it must not be forgotten that only a tiny pro-portion, perhaps 5 per cent of this huge site has been explored for this early period. Four kilometres to the west, however, at the site of Barbar, the remains of a temple complex, which seems to have been founded at the beginning of City II, were found. The lowest levels of Temple I have yielded the same mix of chain-ridged, Umm-an-Nar and Barbar sherds as City IIa (Mortensen 1986: 182). Temple I, which had two phases, was founded on a carefully prepared site with clean blue clay heaped up to form a low mound and then covered with a layer of sand. Round this the platform of the first temple was built, raising the temple above ground level. It was an uneven rectangle measuring 23 to 25 m on two sides and 15 to 17 m on the other two. Andersen states that there was a double platform, of which the lower one, which was badly preserved, was oval and the upper one roughly rectangular. The whole was built of small stones and the upper surface of the platform was heavily plastered. On the rectangular plat-form was a free-standing room, perhaps the shrine, and two groups of rooms, one in the south-west corner and one on the north wall, which seem to be service rooms. At the east end of the platform was a ramp leading to what, in Temple II, became an oval enclosure (Fig. 4.10). In the south-west corner are two flights of steps leading down in the direction of the spring (Andersen 1986: 169, plan).

In the preliminary reports reference is made to eight large cut stone blocks with sockets through them, which may belong to this phase, but Mortensen would put them in the early phase of Temple II (Mortensen 1970: 394). The blocks stand on the lower terrace at right angles to the head of the steps leading down to the spring. Remains of copper sheeting, nails and fragments of wood in the sockets suggest that the blocks supported posts or pillars, possibly to form a processional way. One of the blocks is decorated with figures of stick men, unique for the period, and it has to be asked if they are really contemporary with the use of the blocks in the temple. (A photograph can be seen in Nayeem 1992: 180 Fig. 7).

Much has been made in the past of the Mesopotamian parallels which can be drawn for the purification of the site before building began and also for the superposition of temples on the same spot. The oval shape of the lower platform has also been related to temples dating to the middle of third millennium at sites like Tell al Ubaid, al Hiba

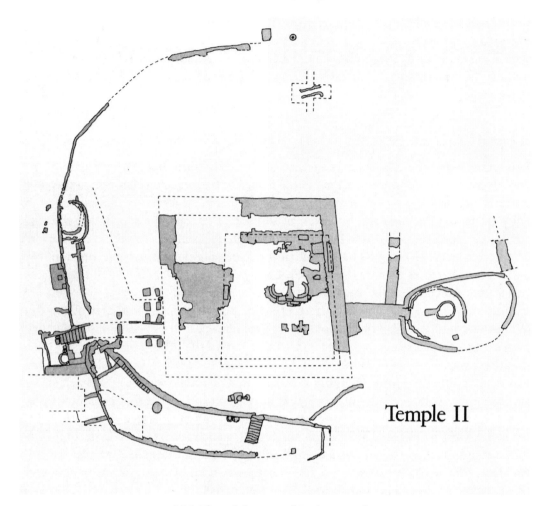

Temple II

4.10 Plan of the second Barbar temple.

and Khafaje in Sumer (Crawford 1991 for a summary). These similarities should not be overemphasized. In Sumer the foundation ritual entailed digging out a deep hole and filling it with clean material, not piling up a mound of clean clay, something which is arguably closer to Egyptian practice; the superposition of sacred buildings can be seen in many cultures in every part of the world and relates to the numinosity of certain spots, or certain springs, as in the case of the Barbar temple. Many Christian churches in the West today rest on the remains of pre-Christian shrines and the Ka'aba itself is said to be on the site of a pre-Islamic holy place. In addition, the parallels between the building and the oval temples of Sumer are of a fairly general nature and cannot be sustained in detail. The Barbar temple is, more probably, an expression of the imagination and skills of the local builders and owes little to any other culture.

The Barbar temple was completely remodelled (Mortensen 1986: 182) at a period contemporary with period IIb at the Qala'at. The double platform was greatly enlarged with the upper one now measuring 26 × 27 m at its maximum. The sacred spring was certainly included in the temple precinct and Andersen has suggested that the well chamber, which was in two parts, may have been covered. He also suggests that the eight squared blocks with sockets in them, belong to the last phase of Temple II and formed a processional way from the well up onto the platform, but as we have seen they lie at right angles to the stair rather than parallel with it (Andersen 1986: 170, plan 38). On the upper platform, which was again on two levels, various installations were uncovered on the higher part. They included a fine, double circular enclosure which may have been an offering place, or altar, and three round-topped stones with holes through the rounded top which have been variously interpreted as tethering places for sacrificial animals or anchors. The obvious importance of the sea to the people of Dilmun makes this latter an attractive idea.

The final features of Temple II to be noted are an oval enclosure on the eastern side of the platform joined to it by a ramp, a pillar on the lower platform and a group of altars west of the well. The oval enclosure also contained a large altar and was covered with fine grey ash, suggesting that it was a place of sacrifice. A large channel or drain was identified east of the enclosure, perhaps to dispose of liquid waste (Andersen 1986: 172). An earlier, circular enclosure lay below the oval one. The pillar, of which only two drum-shaped segments remain, stands today on the lower terrace close to the stair on the south of the temple. The three altars, or podia, stand west of the well against the outer face of the oval platform, but their date is unclear.

The stonework of the platform and the well chamber is of a high standard and in contrast to the small, unworked local stones used in Temple I, the walls of Temple II were faced with better quality stone brought in from Jiddah, a small offshore island to the west. The stone is well-dressed and cut into blocks which are tailored to shape with considerable skill to form a tightly-fitting, smooth surface. The techniques used are very similar to those seen in the stone tombs of Umm-an-Nar and it has been suggested that the masons who built the temple may have come from the mainland as such stone-cutting does not seem to be an indigenous skill in Bahrain (Doe 1986: 191). If this is the case, then it surely tells us something about the level of prosperity and the organization of the people who were rebuilding the Barbar temple. They were capable of transporting both materials and craftsmen from outside the island, and of recompensing them. It also suggests close ties with the Oman peninsula or Umm-an-Nar island.

A number of objects were found associated with the building of this temple, apparently as foundation deposits. They include a copper statuette of a man 13.5cm high, holding his hands before him in an attitude of prayer. It is now thought that, although the figure has some similarities to votive statues from Mesopotamia, the

4.11 Copper bull's head from the Barbar temple.

closest parallels come from the Indo–Iranian borders, or even from Bactria, where somewhat similar figures form the handles of copper mirrors. The connection with Bactria is also suggested by another piece, a copper figure of a bird, slightly smaller than the male figure, which can be compared to bird figures on so-called spatulae from the same area (Pottier 1984). The most spectacular piece is a bull's head, also of copper, rather smaller than life size, with fine sweeping horns and a rather pig-like snout (Fig. 4.11). It too can be compared to heads from Mesopotamia, but some features, notably the treatment of the nose, are also to be found with the bull's head from Altyn Depe in Turkmenistan which also dates to the late third or early second millennia (Mus. Cat.: 30–1). Three cylindrical vases of creamy banded calcite, said to come from the same deposit, are also identical in material and form to ones made at Altyn Tepe (Kohl 1984). It should be noted that there is some discrepancy in the dating of these objects and the Ministry of Information's guide to the Temple states that the alabaster vessels and the bull's head come from Temple III. Potts places them all in Temple II (Potts 1990: 204–5 quoting Mortensen 1986). Another stone vase with a lid has no obvious parallels.

The guide also states that all the Dilmun seals from Barbar were found in Temple III and this, too, is contradicted by Mortensen who places a number of them in Temple

IIb. There is also a sherd with an impression of a Dilmun seal on it showing the so-called Master of the Animals, which came, like several of the seals, from the sacred well (*Ministry Guide*: 39–40). The presence of the seals in the temple may suggest that the temple in Dilmun, as in other parts of the ancient Near East, had administrative and commercial functions. On the other hand, the finds of seals in the well may reflect some ritual where such objects were deposited to bring prosperity or good luck. Even today people find it hard to resist throwing coins into a well or fountain.

A date in the early years of the second millennium is suggested by a pair of C14 dates from the last phase of Temple II which give dates of 2035 and 2070±100 (calibrated), as well as by the close parallels between the pottery from this level and that from City IIb. As Dilmun seals are also found in the succeeding Temple III it seems likely that this rebuilding should be placed as close as possible to late Temple II, perhaps about 1900 BC (Mortensen 1986: 185). It is less clear how long this last period of the Barbar temple may have lasted. The pottery is said to show some Kassite characteristics, which might suggest a latest date *c*. 1500 BC for its abandonment. This would seem too late. There are also seals of Kjaerum's type Ib seals which he places in the Old Babylonian period, *c*. 1800–1600 BC (Kjaerum 1980) and this may be a more realistic date for the abandonment of the site.

The architecture of Temple III is markedly different from that of the earlier temples although it is built on top of the remains of Temple II and has been so badly robbed that little other than the heavy retaining wall of a right-angled platform measuring 38 x 38m has survived. The stair to the well was rebuilt, so some continuity can be traced with the earlier building, but the entrance seems to have been on the north where two more large socket stones were uncovered. There is no evidence that the oval enclosure to the east continued. The surface of the platform is lost so nothing can be said about the buildings which may once have stood on it.

For the first time we have evidence for a second temple at Barbar, the North-East temple, also badly damaged, but apparently showing traces of an upper and a lower platform, the upper one being a perfect square measuring 24 x 24m. No buildings have survived on the surface of the upper platform of this temple either. Finally, today, a single standing stone can be seen standing outside the temple enclosure. It has been re-erected here from Zellac and has no connection with the temple at all. Even its date is uncertain. The scatter of pottery in the date gardens which surround the temple today and unpublished explorations in what is now a car park south of the temple, (Rice pers. comm.) strongly suggest that there was a settlement of some size associated with it.

At least three other temple buildings contemporary with Temple II have been identified in the fertile north of Bahrain. The finest is at Saar where, as has been described earlier, the building stood on the highest point of the site (Fig. 4.12). From here it would have been visible for a considerable distance by land and sea. It is a trapezoidal

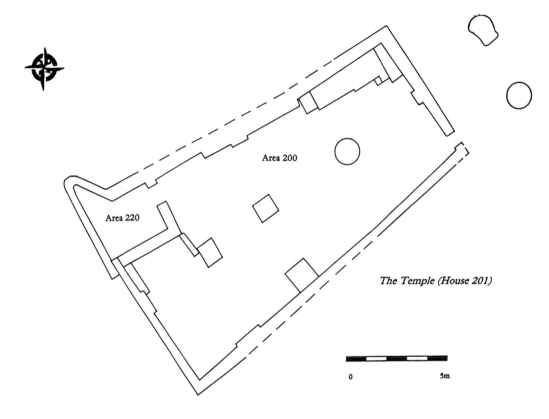

Area 200

Area 220

The Temple (House 201)

0   5m

4.12 The early phase of the Saar temple.

building about seventeen metres long, with the walls facing to the points of the compass built of rough, locally available stone heavily plastered inside and out. The rather small, undecorated entrance stood in the south-east corner. The roof was supported on three stone pillars placed on the long axis of the building. Originally two were square and the easterly one round, but a later remodelling added a skirt to the central pillar so that it too looked round. A storage area lay at the west end of the building. There seem to have been no particular foundations laid for the first temple, but the major rebuild which took place at the end of its lifetime was preceded by the laying down of a thick layer of clean sand on which the renovations were erected. This recalls the foundations of the first Barbar temple, as well as those of the Sin Temple at Khafaje (Crawford *et al.* 1997).

The fixtures and fittings at Saar included an altar on the south wall with a horizontal, crescent-shaped support built against the wall behind it and a second similar one which was built against the north face of the central pillar in the second phase

4.13 The altars in the temple at Saar.

of the temple, after the renovations (Fig. 4.13). Thick deposits of ash were found associated with both the altars with the remains of plants and fishbone in them. It seems reasonable to suggest that these were from food offerings presented to the gods. The presence of two internal altars suggests the possibility that more than one deity may have been worshipped here, but we have no clue as to their identity unless the crescent-shaped supports behind the altars can be taken to suggest moon deities. A series of finely plastered platforms stood against the north and east walls and were remodelled a number of times. It was in this area that fragments of plaster with purple paint on them were found suggesting that the original appearance of the interior was strikingly colourful. Outside the building to the east there is also evidence for two main building periods. Two pillars or altars, one a curious keyhole shape, were placed in front of the temple during its initial phase and were later superseded by five more.

An interesting, but incomplete building, identified by the excavator as a temple, was also found at Diraz, associated with what must have been a considerable settlement, now, sadly, destroyed by developers. At its greatest extent the settlement seems to have stretched from the temple north to the spring at Umm-es-Sejur, a distance of about half a kilometre. The building, which is said to have stood on a low platform, apparently consisted of three sections, a rectangular room to the west, perhaps from the associated finds a work area, and then a portico supported by two rows each of four pillars with a square altar between them. The pillars are made of small stones held together by plaster and the construction technique is the same as that used at Saar. The possibility that the pillars originally supported a roof cannot be ruled out. The final section is a second room to the east of the portico which is 4.5 m long and contains another altar. Beyond this is a first millennium tomb. This reconstruction of the temple plan is somewhat hypothetical as the stratigraphy was very disturbed. The excavation is still unpublished and so it is not possible to be certain that all three parts of the building were in use at the same time.

The pottery associated with the building was mainly of the typical red-ridged Barbar type and a single Dilmun seal was found associated with a secondary wall against the north-east corner of the western room. Apart from this, a variety of house-hold rubbish was retrieved from outside the 'temple precinct' including two steatite lids, animal and fish bone, stone tools and the remains of bitumened baskets (Roaf unpublished report 1978).

Slightly north of the Diraz temple is the spring called Umm-es-Sejour which has already been mentioned in connection with the early evidence for irrigation. Preliminary work here by Bibby in 1954 uncovered a stair leading down to a small enclosure in which was a fine stone well-head on the eastern edge of the pool. The headless remains of two animal statues were found, one still sitting on guard on the steps, the other in the well chamber. These animals are sometimes called rams, but have long thin beards or trunks. It is probable that they are composite animals and should be compared to two similar examples from Mohenjo-Daro, one with a very similar 'trunk' (During-Caspers 1986: 300–1). The figures from Mohenjo-Daro were found in Harappan levels (Allchin and Allchin 1982: 204, Fig. 8.9). The site at Umm-es-Sejour was interpreted by Bibby as a shrine, perhaps part of a temple similar to that at Barbar, partly on the basis of the large numbers of well-finished stone blocks which still today lie on the edge of the pool. It is very possible that these relate not to a second millennium shrine, but to the buildings which are said to have stood there in the historic period and to have been destroyed by the Caliph Abdul al-Malik bin Marwan. The Japanese expedition working at the site found no evidence for the presence of monumental architecture in the Early Dilmun period (Konishi 1994).

Finally, mention must be made of a most unusual and interesting building found on the island of Failaka and also dating to this period. It was found on Tell F6 and stands on a rectangular stone platform. The building is approximately 20 m square, with heavily revetted outer walls, also of stone. The entrance was probably on the south, and gave access to a paved courtyard in which were two rooms and a number of other features. The two rooms lie in the centre of the east and west walls respectively; that on the west wall is subdivided into two uneven parts, the smaller, more westerly one of which may have supported a staircase. In the larger was a sunken tank, presumably for water storage. The room on the eastern side of the court is larger and a number of copper artefacts including a tripod were found in the undisturbed part of the room (Calvet and Gachet 1990). Another sunken basin was found against the north wall of the court and a well-constructed drain ran out under the north wall. The building is dated by the presence of classic Dilmun seals. The probability that this building is a temple is enhanced by the evidence from the lowest levels which shows that it was built on foundations of clean sand laid in a specially prepared pit (Calvet and Gachet 1990: 104).

Other suggestions for its function have included the suggestion that it may have been the base for a great lighthouse at the mouth of the bay. Certainly the size and solidity of the base suggests that the original building must have risen to a considerable height and, as we have seen, there is also evidence for the presence of a stair. The question must remain open.

The well in the Barbar temple and the shrine at Umm-es-Sejour both suggest that sweet water had an important part to play in the life and religion of Dilmun, a suggestion which is supported by the image of Dilmun as a garden paradise painted in the myths of Mesopotamia and especially in the myth of Enki and Ninhursag. Water almost always holds a special place in the lives of people living in a semi-arid environment such as that of Dilmun. Apart from this, it is hard to say much about the religion of the early Dilmun period. The cuneiform texts give us the names of a pair of deities, Inzak and Meskilak whose worship may have been associated with fertility and Inzak certainly had a significance beyond Dilmun itself as a temple was built for his worship in Susa (Vallat 1983). The variety of temple plans which have survived may indicate the worship of a number of different deities, but their nature is unknown. It is also clear from the evidence of the burial mounds that the people of Dilmun believed in an after life which was probably somewhat similar to that on earth. The dead seem to have required food and drink as well as other possessions.

The evidence from the settlements of the Early Dilmun period indicates a number of important changes from the late third millennium, the most significant of which is the shift in the focus of power from the Eastern Province of Arabia to the Bahrain islands. The settlement at Failaka is also founded during this period. There is evidence for a considerable increase in population and for a real increase in material prosperity indicated by the first firm evidence for monumental buildings in the region. All are apparently religious in character except for the protective wall around the main settlement at the Qala'at al Bahrain. The regular nature of the housing at Saar has been taken to suggest some form of central control, but the architectural evidence gives us few clues as to who was wielding that control. The evidence from the graves discussed in the next chapter suggests a possible answer.

Chapter 5

DILMUN: GRAVES AND ARTEFACTS

There is no evidence for burial in the houses of the Dilmun period, all the graves which have been investigated lie outside the settlements in areas set aside for the purpose. In Bahrain the mounds of the early second millennium are concentrated on the rocky limestone outcrops which are unsuitable for agriculture, thus conserving the limited fertile land for agricultural purposes. Later mounds, like those at Jannusan, are also found in the fertile northern strip, as are a number of subterranean graves with no mounds like those found at al Hajjar (Rice 1988). Ibrahim classified the mound burials into five main groups in the course of his work on the very extensive burial fields at Saar and he has listed them as follows: mounds with single burial above ground; mounds with a single burial cut into the bedrock; mounds with central burial connected to subsidiary ones (Fig. 5.1); mounds with shaft entrance; burial complex (Ibrahim 1982: 7). As many as 15,000 mounds may have stood on the Saar ridge at one time. In addition to Ibrahim's types the outstandingly large two-storey mounds, known as the Royal mounds at A'ali and the 'pseudo Umm-an-Nar' graves mentioned in chapter 3, should also be noted.

There does not seem to have been a straightforward chronological relationship between these different types and several were apparently in use together. For example, the magnificent grave complexes at Saar (see Fig. 3.10), which each resemble an enormous honeycomb made of stone with a burial chamber in each cell of the comb, have been interpreted as a development from the single mounds with subsidiary burials, but are probably contemporary with them. The larger of the two complexes at Saar consists of more than 200 burials, the great majority of which date to the Early Dilmun period, though intrusive Kassite burials are found (Mughal 1983: 322), and some of the finds, such as a very fine steatite Hut pot, on display in the National Museum (Crawford and al Sindi 1996), are third-millennium in date. The single graves with subsidiary burials also in the main date to the Early Dilmun period.

All the mounds are built of local stone, often unworked, but occasionally finely shaped. In one type the central chamber was constructed first and the walls seem to have been shored up by a pile of rubble, which was raised as the walls of the tomb chamber grew, making the fitting of the capstones over the chamber much easier. The chamber itself is usually rectangular and large enough to accommodate the slightly crouched body of a single person with a few pots and other gifts. Some of the chambers have up to four alcoves on one or both sides of the chamber in which offerings

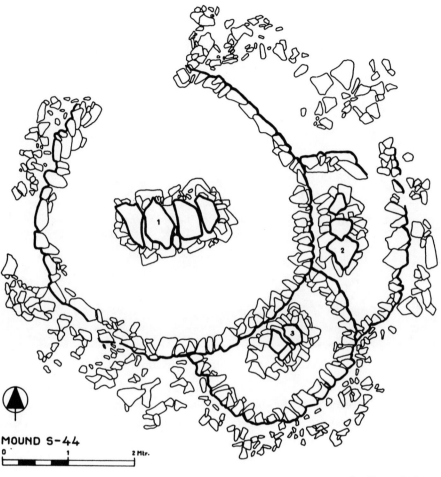

1. Ground plan

5.1 A single grave with subsidiary burials from Saar.

seem to have been placed. The ring wall was then built to the desired height around the chamber and as it rose more packing was tipped from the top of the wall into the centre until the chamber was completely covered (for example Ibrahim 1982: 116 Fig. 7).

A different technique can be seen in a number of graves at Saar one of which was recently reconstructed (Fig. 5.2). The ring wall of worked stone was originally free-standing on the outside and more than two metres high, giving the tomb a cylindrical appearance. The interior of the 'drum' was filled with earth and rubble so that the chambers were again covered. In this particular case a number of subsidiary chambers had also been included inside the ring wall. In other examples, subsidiary graves are

5.2 A reconstructed 'drum' grave from Saar.

built up against the outside of the main ring wall making miniature complexes. Bones are usually poorly preserved so it is normally not possible to tell the age and sex of the burials. However, it would seem that the remains of men, women and children are found and if we assume that people buried together had a close connection in life as well, we can suggest on this basis that those graves containing fewer than ten bodies may well represent the remains of a nuclear family. It is tempting to suggest that the complexes are the burial places of much larger groups such as clans or extended families.

There has been much discussion about the building of these graves and it has been suggested that there may have been a specialized group of tomb builders, but as yet the proof is lacking. Similar skills are now known to have been employed in the building of houses and public buildings, so perhaps we should consider the possibility that there was a class of professional masons who built both tombs and buildings for the living. Looking at the regular plan of the main grave complex at Saar (Ibrahim 1982; Mughal 1983), it does seem possible that it was laid out to a master plan of some sort, which would be another indication of the presence of professional builders. If such a blueprint existed, all the cells need not have been constructed at the same time. If they had been, access to the centre of the complex would have been extremely difficult for the first burial parties.

5.3 A subterranean grave at al Hajjar.

A rather different burial area was uncovered at al Hajjar south of the Budaiya highway and again underlines two important characteristics, the variety of the burial rites apparently in use at the same time, and the chronological confusion introduced by the practice of reutilizing the graves over a very long period of time. The burial chambers at al Hajjar are subterranean, each one having a low wall round it to support the capstones which were usually cemented into position (Fig. 5.3). The interior of the tomb chambers is also often plastered (Rice 1988: 80). The use of plaster is not reported by Ibrahim at Saar, but can still be seen in some of the excavated examples there whose date it is now difficult to establish. It is possible that the al Hajjar graves were first used in the early third millennium as a Jemdat Nasr style seal was recovered from Grave 1, but Porada was of the opinion that it had been recut and so may have been an antique when first deposited in the grave. Other artefacts from the same grave include two Dilmun seals and one described as being like the common seals of Nuzi. These finds would certainly support a second millennium date (Rice 1988: 81).

Almost all the al Hajjar graves were re-used in either the Kassite or even the

Hellenistic period, though fortunately, one grave from al Hajjar 2 was found undisturbed. The body lay on its side in a slightly flexed position with the hands raised in front of the face. A Dilmun seal lay in a position which suggested that it had hung round the person's neck and a small inverted bowl lay close by. Seals have also been found in graves at Saar and in at least one instance have been found in both female and children's graves (Ibrahim 1982 graves S137.3 and S267.4), suggesting that their use was not confined to the male members of society, though they are also found in graves containing spearheads (for example Saar sector D graves 3, 7, 53, and 91, Mughal 1983). Seals are also found with graves with few if any other grave goods and so do not appear to have been used only by the wealthy (Mughal 1983 graves 4 and 139). Only one seal is found in each burial, as one would expect if they were used as signatures.

Generally speaking, the graves in Bahrain are modestly equipped. Most have a piece of pottery, most commonly the 'grave pots' made of a reddish fabric with an ovoid body and ridged neck (see Fig. 3.9), but other shapes and wares also occur. Pottery goblets with Iranian affinities are found and so are occasional sherds of Harappan pottery (Frifelt 1986: 131). Food remains are represented by animal bones, shells, which are also used as cosmetics containers, and perhaps by the remains of bitumened baskets which may have contained bread or fruit. Apart from these essentials, offerings are usually confined to a few scraps of metal, often too corroded to be identified, although spears, knives and arrows have been recovered. More exotic goods include the remains of ostrich egg cups, fragments of ivory, steatite containers and simple pieces of jewellery. Precious metals are rarely found. One grave at Saar was found to contain a pan balance of a type used by pearl merchants on the island until very recently, together with a set of bullet shaped haematite weights now on show in the Bahrain National Museum.

Many of the mounds on the island have been robbed and many more opened by curious amateurs. The information such mounds can give us, even when the finds have survived, is limited. One such group of material has been catalogued by E. During-Caspers and can be used to fill in our picture of the grave goods found in tombs of the Dilmun period. A footed painted goblet of the type referred to before from City II was found in the so-called Jefferson mound at Hamala North, together with a copper version, which also seems to have its nearest parallels in Iran (Fig. 5.4). From the same grave comes a delightful, but badly corroded, little copper figure of a goat, now in the British Museum, 2 cm high with a flicked up tail, and a suspension loop. We do not, of course, know if it was made on the island, but it indicates a high level of technical proficiency (During-Caspers 1980 Pls. V, VI.2 and VII.2). The figure can be compared to various pieces from the Oman peninsula, notably a fine piece of jewellery from Qattarah which shows two similar animals on a pectoral or pendant. This piece is dated to the early second millennium Wadi Suq period (Potts 1990: 253–4).

Finally, we must look at the small group of very large grave mounds from A'ali which have attracted the attention of archaeologists and amateurs since the end of the nine-

5.4 A copper goblet in the National Museum, Bahrain.

teenth century. Today they form all that remains of what was originally an extensive mound field in and around the modern village. They have been much diminished by quarrying and other activities, but in spite of this, the largest still stand more than 12 m high and have a diameter at base of *c.* 30 m. These graves stand out both by reason of their immense size and by the fragmentary remains of grave goods of a much more sumptuous kind. Inside, the largest mounds have double burial chambers placed one above the other with the entrance to the lower one through a stone-lined entrance passage. The lower chamber is partially carved out of the bedrock, the walls are of untrimmed stone, sometimes with traces of plaster and the roofs of the burial chambers are built of huge slabs of rock roughly cut to size. The engineering skills employed to raise these into position must have been considerable, even with unlimited manpower. In terms of the human energy expended on their construction these graves were clearly intended to house an extraordinary group of people.

The fragmentary remains of their contents confirm this hypothesis. Ivory pieces, mostly very broken, are common and include fragments of an ivory box, a bull's leg, perhaps part of a piece of furniture and a fine female figure now in the British Museum (Reade and Burleigh 1978). Ivory 'wands' of a type known from the Indus valley are also mentioned. Other high status finds include a small gold ornament in the shape of a quadruple spiral, which has parallels all across the ancient Near East from Troy to Central Asia, while painted goblets point to connections with Eastern Iran and Baluchistan. The date of these graves is, as usual, difficult to establish, but the presence of the painted pottery goblets, of one or two Wadi Suq pieces, and of typical Early Dilmun pottery, places at least some of them in the first quarter of the second millennium, contemporary with City II and the later phases of the Barbar temple.

The burial mounds provide us with extremely valuable information on the island's history. A study of their distribution, based on the assumption that each mound field was associated with a major settlement, has suggested to Højlund that the island was divided into eight districts at the height of its prosperity in the early second millennium (Højlund 1989a: 48–9). Based on a reference in a text from Mari to a king of Dilmun, he further suggests that these districts were combined into a state under a king. The evidence for eight administrative areas is lacking, but the association between a mound field and a settlement can certainly be demonstrated at Saar and probably at Umm Jidr (Cleuziou 1981) where a Barbar period settlement has been reported within the al Areen wildlife park. No settlement has yet been found near Aʿali, where, on the basis of the graves, one might expect a substantial town, and no grave mounds occur near the Qalaʿat, so we do not know where the inhabitants of City II were buried. This has led scholars to suggest that the al Hajjar field may perhaps have served City II, and the settlement around the Barbar temple, while it has been argued that the so-called Royal graves may house the rulers of City II. These possibilities can only remain speculative until further evidence is available.

THE EASTERN PROVINCE

The close links between Bahrain and the mainland at this time are demonstrated by the enormous mound fields which could still be seen around Dhahran in the early 1980s, lying at the north end of a fertile coastal strip which was inhabited from Ubaid times. When these mounds were first explored there were said to be thousands of graves, but survey in 1983 located only 900 (Zarins 1984: 26). Three types of grave mound were identified, the first of which is similar to many of the Bahrain mounds. This type consists of a central chamber, either above or below ground, covered with capstones and surrounded by a ring wall, the whole being enclosed in a mound. The grave goods, where these survive, also show close links with Bahrain. The red ovoid grave pots with corrugated necks and ridged Barbar pottery are both found, as are examples of Umm-an-Nar and Wadi Suq wares and of the goblets of red or yellowish ware which can be matched in the A'ali graves. There is also said to be a limited amount of early third-millennium ware (Zarins 1984: 32).

Many of the graves had been robbed and repeatedly re-used over a long period of time so that the dating of the surviving contents is often difficult. It is often impossible to be sure how many of the burials belong to the initial period of the grave. Tomb 6 yielded 120 bodies, A5 fifty-two. Parallels with the Bahrain graves would suggest that the original burials were restricted to a limited number of family members. One unpublished Jemdat Nasr stamp seal is reported by Zarins (1984: 37) and one Persian Gulf seal and one classic Early Dilmun have been published (Piesinger 1983: Fig. 186; al Mughannam *et al.*: 1986 Pl. 18a), as well as a shell example with three quadrupeds drilled on it (al Mughannam *et al.* 1986: 10 and Pl. 5). Metal and stone objects are few, although lapis and banded agate beads are reported.

THE MATERIAL CULTURE

The seals

It is now time to look in more detail at the material culture of the Dilmun period, combining the evidence from graves and settlements. The most attractive group of artefacts is the circular stamp seals, the majority of which are made of steatite or chlorite. The first seals occur in the lowest level of the period II settlement at the Qala'at where seals of the so-called Persian (or Arabian) Gulf type were found (Højlund and Andersen 1994: 322). Seals were primarily used for identification, as signatures, as trade marks, as badges of office, and even as credit cards. The appearance of both weights and seals together in period IIa at the Qala'at, with a limited number of seal impressions, is good evidence for the growing importance of trade and commerce on the island at this time and for an increasing administrative sophistication. It has been thought that the Persian Gulf seals predate the classic Dilmun ones, but once again, the stratigraphic evidence is not entirely satisfactory as many either come from graves or have no firm context. In addition to the examples listed by Potts (Potts 1990a: 162–3) a further six have now been published, one from a grave in Hamad town with Indus valley symbols on it (Fig. 5.5) (Srivasavta 1991: 25), and five from the settlement at Saar (Fig. 5.6). The author has also seen a Persian Gulf seal picked up from the surface at Diraz, another site currently attributed to the early second millennium. A second seal in a similar style, probably from this site, is illustrated in the Museum Catalogue, no. 252, while a third, no. 256, seems to belong to a rather later group.

One of the Saar examples was a surface find and so is unstratified. This seal[11] is something of a puzzle as, although the shape and the design are of the Persian Gulf type,

---

[11] S21:0:0, museum no. 4133.

5.5 A Persian Gulf seal with Indus signs from Hamad Town.

there are traces of four dot and circles on the reverse with three parallel lines, a style typical of the Early Dilmun seals. It seems that the perforation has been redrilled, so perhaps this is a Persian Gulf seal which has been re-used with the decoration on the reverse being added when the seal was recycled. Another seal,[12] was found in house 53 which dates to the late phase of the settlement, *c.* 1800 BC which might suggest that the style continued in use longer than is generally supposed. A third[13] from house 208 shows a schematic human figure. Their occurrence in late Early Dilmun period contexts of the nineteenth to eighteenth centuries at Saar suggests that they may have continued in use for rather longer than has previously been thought and that they overlap in time with the Early Dilmun style, rather than merely preceding it. The find of a cuneiform tablet associated with a Persian Gulf seal outside the walls of City II at the Qalaʿat would also point in this direction (Brunswig *et al.* 1983).

[12] registration no. 2262: 05.   [13] registration number 4139: 01.

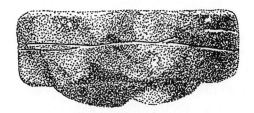

5.6 A Persian Gulf seal from Saar.

A number of Persian Gulf seals have also been found outside Bahrain, but they are not helpful either in trying to establish a clear chronology. The largest collection comes from the Sumerian city of Ur and is, with two exceptions, poorly stratified. One example with a good context, U.8685, comes from grave PG 401, which is not listed in the published catalogue and so is undated, while the other is loosely associated with a grave dated to the Ur III period (PG 1847) (see Mitchell 1986 for a complete catalogue). Another comparable seal comes from level IVB at the site of Tepe Yahya in southern Iran. This level has usually been dated rather earlier, to the middle of the third millennium, a period contemporary with the Intercultural style softstone bowls found at Tarut (Lamberg-Karlovsky 1973: Pl. XXVI). However, Potts is now proposing a later date for this level at Yahya which would agree rather better with the evidence from Bahrain which, as we have seen, suggests that these seals first appeared at the end of the third millennium (Potts 1990).

The seals are often made of a hard, mottled dark greenish stone, rather than the soft-stone used for the Early Dilmun seals, and are circular with a high boss on the reverse, sometimes decorated with one or two grooves. The height of the seal is often more or less the same as its diameter and the profile is usually straight or slightly concave. Stylistically these seals are somewhat crude and the majority show either naturalistic or rather schematic animals, often bulls or gazelle, with filler motifs scattered in a rather haphazard way in the field. Human figures are rare, although a popular motif is a human foot. In contrast to the Dilmun seal the compass drill is not used. About one third of the examples known are distinguished by the use of signs in the Indus valley script as part of the design. The signs can mostly be matched with those known in the Indus (Potts 1990: 166), but Parpola has pointed out that the signs are sometimes found in groupings which do not occur together in the Indus. This suggests to him that the signs represent names in a different language, perhaps that of Dilmun (Brunswig *et al.* 1983: 106). Some of the motifs, notably the humped bull, also show Harappan influence. No Persian Gulf seals have yet been found in the Indus valley, but the later, classic Early Dilmun seals have been found in Harappan levels, for example at Lothal while designs closely related to those from Bahrain can be seen at Mohenjo-Daro (Marshall 1931: Pl. CXII no. 383) and at a second port site, Dwarka (Fig. 5.7) (Chakrabati 1995: 111). The chronological picture remains inconclusive but it seems likely that the Persian Gulf seals are probably in part contemporary with the classic Early Dilmun ones, though they may have been in use slightly earlier. The association of one of these seals with the so-called Amorite tablet from outside the wall of period II at the Qalaʿat supports the evidence from Ur that the style was in use in the late third millennium. They also remained in use through most of the Early Dilmun period and could be the products of a specific workshop rather than a chronological variation, although more stratified examples are needed.

The seals from the upper levels of the Qalaʿat's period II are all of the Early Dilmun

5.7 Seal from the Harappan port of Dwarka.

type. These circular stamp seals are made of the same steatite and are typically larger with a flatter boss than the Persian Gulf ones. They are frequently glazed with a light glaze. The boss is almost always decorated with three incised lines running at right angles to the perforation and four dot and circle motifs made with a compass drill, two on either side of the incised lines. The sides of the seal are often slightly concave, though straight- and convex-sided examples do occur, and the repertoire of designs is much more varied.

Human figures appear commonly for the first time, often with a distinctive jutting chin or beard, and a long skirt rather reminiscent of the fleecy skirts worn by statues of middle and late third-millennium date in Mesopotamia. The figures, usually male, engage in a variety of activities including hunting, feasting and sailing the seas in small boats. There is also a group of erotic scenes. Horned creatures, especially bulls, goats and various types of gazelle, deer and oryx are very popular. The motifs shown on the seals can, in some cases, be related to themes known in Mesopotamia, North Syria, Susa, or even further afield in Central Asia[14] (Fig. 5.8), but the treatment is distinctively different. Techniques of cutting the seals are more varied than those used on the Persian Gulf seals. For example, the compass drill is widely used, not only for the

---

[14] The god drinking from a straw is found in North Syria and wheel of animal heads occurs not only here, but as far away as the Murghab delta in Central Asia (Crawford 1991b).

5.8 Dilmun seals from Saar.

ubiquitous dot and circle motif, but also to delineate the heads and eyes of the horned animals. Kjaerum has also identified a proto-Dilmun style where the back is decorated like the classic Early Dilmun seals, but the motifs are closer to those on the Persian Gulf examples (Kjaerum in Højlund and Andersen 1994).

Examples of the Early Dilmun type of seal, like the Persian Gulf ones, have been found outside the island. The largest collection comes from the island of Failaka at the mouth of Kuwait harbour. Teams of various different nationalities, most notably the French, have been working here since 1972. Their work has uncovered upwards of 500 seals, 65 per cent of which are of the classic Dilmun type. Sadly, many of them were found in secondary contexts, in the fill of later buildings for example, so that their analysis has been solely on stylistic criteria (Kjaerum 1983). In the course of his work Kjaerum has been able to isolate three distinct stylistic groups amongst the Failaka seals of which style Ia, dating to the Early Dilmun period, is predominant (Kjaerum 1980). This is also the style which can be most closely matched amongst the published examples from Bahrain. Style Ib, a more linear style, where the human body is shown in true profile, has also been identified among the seals from Saar now in the process of publication. However, Kjaerum's style II, which is marked by the increasing use of the point drill, and which he dates to the Old Babylonian to Kassite periods, does not occur frequently on Bahrain itself. A few bi-facial seals, decorated in style III, which form a distinctive feature of the Failaka corpus, are illustrated in al Sindi's catalogue of seals in the Bahrain National Museum (al Sindi 1994, in Arabic). The relative dearth of style II examples is surely another indication of the decline in prosperity on Bahrain at the end of the Early Dilmun period. Many of the Failaka seals seem to have been manufactured on that island, recycling fragments of steatite vases, apparently of third-millennium date. The only other workshop so far identified was found in City II levels at the Qala'at al Bahrain (Højlund and Andersen 1994: 337).

Further afield, a few Early Dilmun seals come from Mesopotamia, notably from the site of Ur (Gadd 1932; Mitchell 1986). There is also one example recently published from Ischali in the Diyala valley, dating to the Isin-Larsa period *c.* 2000 BC (Hill and Jacobsen 1990: Pl. 42d). It was found in the treasury of the Inanna/Kititium temple at this site. Further evidence for contacts between the two areas can be seen in a number of Mesopotamian cylinder seals of early second-millennium date, or slightly later, which seem to show elements from the Dilmun repertoire, such as the men with jutting chins (al Gailani-Werr 1986). Similarities in design have also been noted with North Syrian seals of the period. Drinking scenes and certain motifs such as tables with elegant legs ending in bulls' hoofs, can be closely matched (Potts 1986b). The wide distribution of seals with radial designs which occurs in Central Asia and Anatolia as well as in Dilmun has also been discussed (Crawford 1991b). It might be suggested, in this context that a very unusual seal impression found on a sherd from Failaka may perhaps be from a so-called Taip cylinder seal, also of Central Asian origin (Pic in Calvet and Gachet 1990: 138–9 no. 26).

More Dilmun seals come from Susa, which seems to have had regular contacts with Dilmun and where there was a temple dedicated to Inzak, the patron god of Dilmun (Amiet 1986; Harper *et al.* 1992: 19). In Arabia three stamp seals of Persian Gulf and Early Dilmun type, two of stone and one of shell, were found at Dhahran (see p. 50). Another very worn (possibly) Persian Gulf seal was found 'In the open desert near the coast, between the towns of Al Khobar and Damman'. This seal is said to be made of highly silicified chlorite schist, rather than steatite (Barger 1969: 140; and for a photograph Potts 1989). Three seals were found in unstratified contexts near Nadqan, south of Hofuf (Golding 1974) and there is said to be another in a secondary context from the Iron Age site of Fao in Saudi Arabia. From Oman, Cleuziou illustrates one found in a grave at Mazyad (1981: Fig. 8). These finds do not, of course, necessarily imply the presence of Dilmun merchants, or even direct contacts between the areas, but they certainly illustrate the complex network of interrelationships which spanned the ancient world and serve to confirm the dates proposed for the Early Dilmun period.

In addition to the seals themselves, archaeologists have found large numbers of impressions made by these seals when they were used to stamp packages and bundles. The knots in the string used to tie the goods were covered with a lump of clay and the seal was pressed into it so that it could be seen at once if the package had been tampered with. Seal impressions were even used in a similar way to 'lock' doors closed with a lump of clay. There is one type of impression which is particularly interesting and this is a group of small circular 'buttons' or tokens of clay which have an impression on one or both sides. In the later case the impressions are similar but not identical (see for example Crawford 1993: Fig. 12). This particular token bears an arrow symbol on each side which also appears on seals from Failaka and which could be interpreted as proto-writing (Kjaerum 1983) (Fig. 5.9). Some tokens are pierced for suspension. Tokens with identical designs have been found at different sites and this suggests the possibility that they acted as authorizations or identification within some system which covered a number of settlements. For example, two tokens with a design of concentric circles decorated with little loops were found at Saar, while apparently identical ones come from the Barbar temple and the Qalaʿat.

No examples of the Indus valley script have been found on the Early Dilmun type of seal, although the script was still in use in the Indus valley when the seals were in circulation. With the exception of the so-called Amorite tablet previously mentioned, no other tablets have been found in levels of the Early Dilmun period. Occasional fragments of cuneiform have, however, been recovered, such as the jar sherd from period Ib at the Qalaʿat which is inscribed with a measure of capacity (Eidem in Højlund and Andersen 1994: 301). It is hard to believe that the businessmen of Dilmun, in touch through the copper trade with literate people to the north in Mesopotamia and Syria, and to the south in the Indus valley, were not themselves literate. Their involvement in a complex commercial world makes their literacy even more likely as it seems that the need to record economic transactions was the spur to the development of a recording system in Mesopotamia, and possibly in Egypt (Nissen 1993).

If it is accepted that Dilmun probably did have some form of recording system, the lack of archaeological evidence forces us to conclude that the merchants of Dilmun, whatever script they used, probably wrote on perishable materials such as bark or palm leaves. The people of Dilmun may have borrowed the Indus script, just as they seem to have borrowed the Indus system of weights and measures, alternatively, they may have borrowed the flexible cuneiform system, also successfully used in North

5.9 A 'token' from Saar.

Syria for writing languages such as Eblaite, or they may have invented their own. It is a riddle which may never be solved as the environmental conditions are not conducive to the preservation of organic materials. We can only hope for a monumental Dilmunite inscription carved on stone.

The weights used in the economic system are known from a number of sites. Two systems were in use, one derived from the Indus valley and one from Mesopotamia. As we saw earlier, the typical Indus valley weight is a cube, often of brown banded chert. The most commonly occurring weight is 13.5 gm, the base unit is 1.7 gm, and the system is, at least in part, a binary one with ratios of 2:4:8:16:32:64 (Zaccagnini 1986). It is this system which is referred to as the standard of Dilmun in the Ebla texts of the late third millennium, and in Mesopotamia itself, underlining Dilmun's role as a middleman and a channel for both goods and ideas. Archives from the royal palace at the city of Ebla *c.* 2300 BC use the Dilmun shekel as the unit of measurement for pricing metals (Pettinato 1991: 86). Mesopotamian weights were used in Dilmun in addition to the Indus valley ones. A number of highly polished bullet-shaped examples, usually of hard, polished black stone or haematite, and closely similar in form to ones used in Mesopotamia, have been found and one charming duck weight, again of Mesopotamian origin, came from the Dhahran mound field (Piesinger 1983: Fig. 186.7). The Mesopotamian system used a basic unit of 8.5gm, the so-called shekel, sixty of which made a *mina*. A pan balance was found in mound 352 at Saar associated with some of these bullet-shaped weights and is currently on display in the National Museum of Bahrain. It is not unparalleled to have two systems in use together, as seems to have been the case in Dilmun. A similar situation can be seen in Britain today where imperial measures are still battling it out with metric ones.

As well as these high quality stone artefacts, Early Dilmun settlement sites are remarkable for the large quantities of ground stone tools which litter the surfaces. Most were apparently domestic in use, at least at Saar, though at other sites hammerstones may have been used for metalworking and many net weights and sinkers are also found. A variety of stone is used in their manufacture, some local, some apparently of Arabian origin. On the whole the tools from Saar show a correlation between material and function which is probably the result of simple economics; the larger querns and mortars tend to be made of 'cheap' locally available material and are often re-used as door sockets, while smaller pounders and grinders are of scarcer imported stone. It is difficult in some cases to know whether some of the unworn, well-made artefacts were intended as tools or whether they may have been used as weights. Chipped stone is not so commonly found on sites of this date, although the local flint still occurs.

Steatite

Containers of stone are also widely found in early second-millennium contexts in Bahrain and the Eastern Province. The most common material used is that generally referred to under the blanket terms chlorite or steatite, a soft stone widely available, as we have already seen, in Arabia and in Iran (Kohl *et al.* 1979). Vessels made from this material are traditionally divided into three stylistic and chronological groups known as *série ancienne*, *série récente* and *série tardive* (see for example Zarins 1989: 82), but more recently it has been suggested that a *série intermédiaire* should be inserted between the *ancienne* and the *récente* series (for example Potts 1990: 249). The *série ancienne* vases of the third millennium, which include the fine vessels from Tarut elaborately decorated with figurative motifs, are rare on Bahrain, though one or two unpublished sherds have been found recently at Saar. Perhaps the most common forms in these two areas are those which belong to the so-called Omani group of shallow bowls in grey steatite, sometimes with a single trough spout, sometimes with vertically pierced lug handles, decorated with the dot and circle motif in a single row below the rim (Fig. 5.10). Potts would place these in the *série intermédiaire*. Slightly later come a group of conical vessels with concave sides, often with lids. The lids are circular with

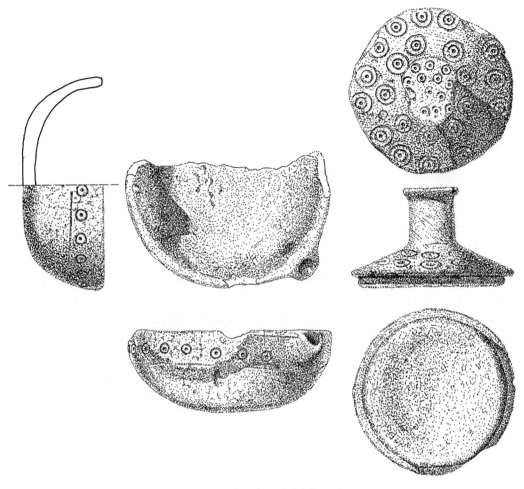

5.10 Steatite bowls and lid from Saar.

an elongated stalk-like handle, topped with a flat knob. Both pots and lids are decorated with increasing numbers of double circles with dots in the centre and a limited
range of linear motifs as well. Some compartmented boxes are also known, but are not
as common as in Oman. It is now generally accepted that many of these *série récente*
vessels originate in Oman and that a number were made at Maysar (Weisgerber 1981).
Some time in the middle of the second millennium herringbone patterns of broken
lines become popular (Häser 1990). There is no evidence for the production of these
bowls in Bahrain, though the workshop on Tarut island may have continued in production into the second millennium. On Failaka the only evidence for the working of
steatite comes from recycling activities, where sherds from third-millennium vessels,
some in the Intercultural style, seem to have been reworked as pendants and beads,

and possibly also as seals (Ciarli 1990). There is also the workshop for beads and seals referred to above from City II.

Pottery

The chain-ridged ware of the pre-Dilmun or Barbar I period dies gradually out, as does the painted Umm-an-Nar ware. The pottery repertoire of the Early Dilmun or Barbar II period is a limited one which develops out of that of the earlier period. The ridged jars, first found in the pre-Dilmun period, with a distinctive red fabric levigated with scraps of limestone which explode into little sun bursts in the firing are ubiquitous. A group of eight ridged, ovoid jars were found by Woolley in the Royal Cemetery at Ur, his types 105/6, and it has been suggested that these jars may be Dilmun in origin. Woolley thought that the jars were foreign (Woolley 1934), but they are firmly dated to the middle of the third millennium by the associated finds, which include seals with the standard Early Dynastic banquet and contest scenes[15] so it is hard to see how they can be derived from Dilmun. Ridged ware only becomes widespread in Bahrain towards the end of the third millennium, three or four hundred years later than the Royal graves. Woolley also describes the ware as thin, brown and hard-fired, not features which characterize Barbar pottery. Another distinctive Early Dilmun shape in a fine red fabric is the so-called grave pot, a round based, straight-sided jar with multiple corrugations on the neck. It is the most commonly found pot in the burial mounds of the period. It was thought that this pot was exclusively used for funerary offerings, but it has now also been found in limited numbers in the settlement at Saar.

Many of the Dilmun period vessels are covered with a yellowish slip, sometimes wiped off in such a way as to resemble ridging. Another group of pots, including wide, flat plates, and jars with strainers built into their necks, are made of a different yellow fabric. It is interesting to speculate on what the strainer jars were used for. The strainer was obviously intended to stop detritus of some sort entering the jar so that the liquid was free of inclusions when served. Perhaps the jugs were used to draw beer from a larger container so that the mash could not get in. Some very large ridged vats in the red fabric have been found in houses at Saar, but were probably used for storing water rather than beer.

Painted pottery is not common, but both local and imported varieties do occur. The decoration is usually geometric, often simple hoops of paint around the upper part of the body, and some can be related to early second-millennium Wadi Suq wares from Oman, while a few pieces are thought to have come from the Indus valley. Some distinctive goblets, in a reddish ware with black paint were found in the lower levels of City II (Mortensen 1986: 180) and in the Royal graves at Aʿali (Mus.Cat.: 23 nos. 31–2).

---

[15] The banquet scene is numbered as U12330 Pl. 194 and the contest scene U12461, Pl. 191.

During-Caspers (1986) has argued convincingly that these cups have their closest parallels with pieces from Baluchistan, although they also occur more widely in the Indo–Iranian borders. There is also a curious group of pots described as canisters, round bottomed jars with a foot or stand built in. Some of these are painted with animal figures and one on display in the National Museum shows a procession of camels (Vine 1993). Others are undecorated like one now in the British museum (BM number 130591.1926.10.8.7). The very distinctive shape of these pots, though not their decoration, can be matched in similar canisters of incised grey ware of Isin-Larsa date from the Diyala valley (Delougaz 1952) and also from Susa. The Mesopotamian and Elamite vessels are decorated with charming, rather crudely drawn pictures of animals and birds, which are filled with white paint. It has been suggested that the shape may have originated in Susa where the greatest numbers have been found, and have been diffused to both Mesopotamia and the Gulf (Hanson 1992). If this could be shown to be the case, it would provide new evidence for the importance of Susa in the international trade of the early second millennium.

Apart from these parallels, it is noticeable that there is little pottery which seems to be of Mesopotamian origin in the Early Dilmun, Barbar II period, less than in the pre-Dilmun period. Conversely, the proportion of wares in the 'Eastern tradition' which, as defined by Højlund, includes wares from Iran, Baluchistan and the Indus, increases slightly, never becoming a major feature of the assemblage. The amount of wheel-turned pottery also increases throughout the period. (For two different views on this cf. Højlund and Andersen 1994 and Heinz 1994.) The uniform nature of the pottery and the limited number of shapes both suggest mass production by professional potters with fairly limited skills, another indication of craft specialization and the increasing complexity of society which accompanies such specialization.

Metalwork

There is very little evidence for the presence of precious metals in Early Dilmun, although the gold bead from A'ali indicates that it was available. Evidence for the working of copper comes from a number of sites on Bahrain in the Early Dilmun period. From the Qala'at come ingots, crucibles and moulds, the majority from City Ib, all apparently used for simple copper artefacts made in an open mould or from copper sheeting. These include blades, pins, fish hooks and simple finger rings (Højlund 1994: 377). Some more sophisticated artefacts are also known too, such as the socketed spearheads of which an example also comes from period Ib at the Qala'at. More recently a very similar one was found at the Saar settlement, and a large hoe with the blade at a right angle to the socket was also recovered from one of the houses. Analysis of the metal deposits in the crucibles at the Qala'at found that the pattern of impurities matched that found in the nickel-rich ores of the Oman peninsula (Northover in

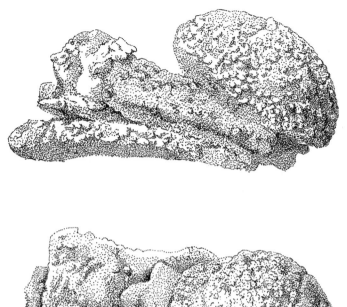

5.11 A copper bun ingot from Saar.

Højlund and Andersen 1994: 375). The crucibles were apparently used for melting the metal, not for smelting it. The smelting would have been carried out nearer to source to minimize the weight of the metal being transported overseas. Timber for stoking the fires was also more freely available in the region of the mines.

There is unpublished evidence from a site called Nasiriyah on the west coast of Bahrain, south of Zellac, for another copper-working area and ingots from here are displayed in the National Museum (Soweilah pers. comm.). At Saar, too, the typical bun-shaped ingots (Fig. 5.11) have been found with the same range of simple tools such as fish-hooks, a hoe and chisels (Fig. 5.12). A fine awl was recovered in 1995 still with its bone handle largely intact. A copper-working kiln was apparently uncovered in one of the houses towards the south end of the main road by the Bahraini/Jordanian

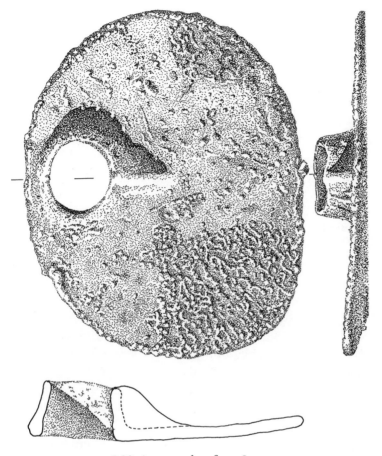

5.12 A copper hoe from Saar.

expedition, but this too remains unpublished. The recycling of copper scrap is also said to have taken place on Failaka (Calvet 1984: 58). There is little evidence for the working of any other metals in Dilmun at this period, or for the use of sophisticated casting techniques such as *cire perdue*. The objects made by this technique such as a handle in the shape of a male figure from the Barbar temple are probably imports. Sheet metal was also available, but the pieces are usually so fragmentary that it is difficult to know what they were used for. The evidence of the artefacts suggests that we are not looking at anything more sophisticated than a cottage industry.

Miscellanea

Other artefacts were made of perishable materials like reeds and palm fronds of which the ghost sometimes remains on the surface of the bitumen with which they were sometimes coated. Occasional impressions of textiles also survive. Shells were used as beads, as containers, for seals, and perhaps also as lamps. In all there is little evidence for the production of any form of luxury goods, unless the seals can be put in this category although they also had a strictly practical function. Beads are perhaps the exception and are found in a wide range of materials including pottery, frit, lapis and carnelian. Bibby reports turquoise, or turquoise faience beads from City I at the Qala'at, while those from City II were almost all carnelian (Bibby 1986: 111). Some plain bitumen beads were found at Saar. Of these materials, only some of the shells and perhaps the bitumen, are locally available so that it seems probable that most of the beads found were imports. Lapis and turquoise may have come by sea up the Gulf from Afghanistan and north-eastern Iran, via the Indus valley, while the carnelian may have originated in the Indus, though other sources are known east of Bushire on the Iranian coast (Potts. T. 1994).

SUMMARY

This survey of the material culture of Dilmun in the first quarter of the second millennium and of its burial customs suggests certain features which apparently characterized its social organization. A diverse population on the island is indicated by the range of burial practices in use at the beginning of the second millennium, but all the types of burial have pottery and other grave goods in common. These two observations taken together seem to indicate the presence of peoples with different cultural traditions and perhaps different geographical origins, united in their material culture by proximity. People tend to be extremely conservative in their method of burial and continue to use their traditional practices, even when living in a different environment. The similarity of the grave goods in all the different types of graves suggests that, whatever their origins, these groups formed a coherent cultural unit by the early second millennium. There is no evidence that any of the burials described were those of foreigners from Mesopotamia or the Indus valley. Such graves could be expected to contain some exotic elements. We can suggest instead that the Bahrain islands of four thousand years ago may have resembled the islands of today where people originally from both shores of the Gulf and from further afield, with different traditions, have become amalgamated into Bahraini society. The situation in the Eastern Province is rather different, the wide range of burial practices does not seem to occur, perhaps pointing to a less diverse society.
    It has already been remarked that the individual grave mounds with under a dozen burials may have belonged to nuclear families, while the large grave complexes may be the burial places of extended family groups or clans, further evidence perhaps of social diversification, although all types contain broadly the same range of goods. We must also bear in mind the possibility that the burial mounds only represent the urban

population, or the wealthier members of society, and that many may not have had the resources to build such monuments. Other simpler methods for the disposal of the dead may have been used for the poorer members of society, like throwing bodies into the sea, which have left no trace in the archaeological record.

The contents of the burials do not indicate a highly stratified society, although some craft specialists must have been present within the society. The presence of specialist masons, for instance, seems highly probable, and of priests to serve the temples (see chapter 8). Pottery was also mass-produced and the engraving of seals must have demanded a high level of technical proficiency, but there is little other indication of craft specialization or of differences in status in the graves. Most people seem to have been buried with the same limited range of goods and in the few cases where the age and sex of the body can be determined, it seems that men and women were treated in a similar fashion. (The poor preservation of bone makes detailed demographic studies almost impossible.) It is only the size and nature of the funerary monument which varies.

The one exception to this generalization is provided by the Royal graves at A'ali. Their size, the labour which was invested in building them, and the comparative richness of what remains of their contents make it probable that these graves represent the burials of a very special group within the society, but at present, we have little indication of its nature. We do not know if this group was made up of rulers, priests, or extremely successful merchants. The only clue comes from a small number of references to the King of Dilmun in texts from Mari of early second-millennium date (Groneberg 1992). If these references can be substantiated then the burials at A'ali must surely be those of the rulers and their families.

Chapter 6

THE OMAN PENINSULA: SETTLEMENT AND ARCHITECTURE

Most of the evidence we have considered so far has come from Eastern Arabia and the adjacent islands, but Dilmun was not the only foreign country with which southern Mesopotamia forged important commercial links. From the early Agade period, *c.* 2350 BC, Magan enters the world scene. Sargon of Agade boasted in his famous inscription of the ships of Magan coming to the quays of Agade, together with those from Dilmun and Meluhha, while his successors almost all showed a rather predatory interest in it. Rimush and Manishtusu campaigned against it while Naram-Sin claims not only to have mined diorite for his royal statues in Magan, but to have campaigned against it and won a great victory (Potts T. 1994: 113).

As in the case of Dilmun there has been much scholarly debate about the exact location of Magan and although some uncertainties remain, it seems likely that, as we have seen with Dilmun, the name was applied to different areas at different times. In the Agade inscriptions, when the name first appears, Magan is apparently used for the Iranian coast of the Gulf rather than the Arabian one (Glassner 1989). It is certainly hard to believe that an Akkadian army under Naram-Sin could have been transported to the Oman peninsula, but by the early second millennium the name does seem to refer to this area. At some periods in history the name may have applied to parts of both the Arabian and the Iranian coast. On a map of 1862–3 published by Palgrave (1883) with his account of his travels in Arabia the Persian coast of the straits of Hormuz is marked as 'Belonging to Oman', underlining the close relationship between the two sides of the Gulf.

The area of ancient Magan is today covered by the modern states of the United Arab Emirates and Oman itself. It is geographically diverse and much richer in raw materials than its neighbour Eastern Arabia (Tosi 1975). Contact between these two regions is not particularly easy by land and there can be little doubt this was an important factor in explaining the distinctive character of the material cultures which developed in the two regions. An established land route links Hofuf in Eastern Arabia with Qatar, but Lorimer describes the 200-mile route as having poor water and no supplies along the way (Lorimer 1908 repr. 1970: 672). From Qatar a route runs east along the coastal strip, but contact by sea, using the shelter offered by the string of offshore islands like Dalma and Sir Bani Yas, and harbours at Umm-an-Nar and other similar locations, was easier and faster, especially for the transport of goods in bulk. It has already been noted (see chapter 1 and de Cardi 1978: 17) that the sea-level was perhaps as much as two metres higher in the third millennium on this coast, suggesting that anchorages were better and more widely distributed than they are today. Such contact as existed between the two areas must surely have been by sea.

In geographical terms the Oman peninsula can be roughly divided into three main areas, the northern coastal strip from Qatar to the Musandam; the area east of the great mountain range of the Hajar al Gharbi, which includes the fertile Batinah coast; and the western slopes of the mountain range where runoff has created a series of oases which also have access to the rich mineral resources of the mountains. These resources include lead and silver, but above all sulphide coppers, which seem to have been exploited from the late fourth millennium until the Islamic period (Hauptmann *et al.* 1988). In addition there are high quality stones such as diorite, a variety of softstones and semi-precious stones such as jasper and carnelian, which is also found near Bushire on the Iranian coast (Whitehouse 1975: 130). It is from these oases and along the routes linking them to each other and to the sea that the earliest evidence of permanent settlement comes.

The major routes across the mountain range are limited; the most northerly links the area around Sharjah with the Indian Ocean and the Fujairah area; just north of this lies the wadi Asimah (Vogt 1994) an important early mining area; the next major route joins the great Buraimi oasis, where Hili is situated today, via the copper-rich wadi Jizzi with the east coast at Sohar. Buraimi is an important crossroads as several other routes link it with the north coast, one running north-west to Abu Dhabi, one northeast to Sharjar and another further north to Ras al Khaimah. The end of two of these paths is marked by important third-millennium sites at Umm-an-Nar island and Tell Abraq respectively (Fig. 6.1). A third-millennium site has also been reported at a site adjacent to Abu Dhabi International Airport at a spot on the mainland close to Umm-an-Nar island.[16] The relative importance of these access routes to the sea seems to have fluctuated through time and Abraq continues to be an important centre after Umm-an-Nar was deserted (Potts 1990b). About eighty-five miles further south of the wadi Jizzi another important wadi crosses the mountains to link the oasis of Ibri to the coast close to Sur; the fourth major crossing point uses the wadi Sama'il near Nizwa to join the interior to the coast near Muscat. This area, which marks the northern end of the Sharqiyah, also ultimately gives a second route to the Indian Ocean in the far south.

THE ECONOMY

As in Eastern Arabia, fishing, hunting and farming all seem to have played an important part in the economy of the region, but the extraction of metals and the smelting of copper also provided vital and profitable resources. It seems reasonable to suggest

---

[16] I am grateful to Peter Hellyer of the Abu Dhabi Islands Survey for this information.

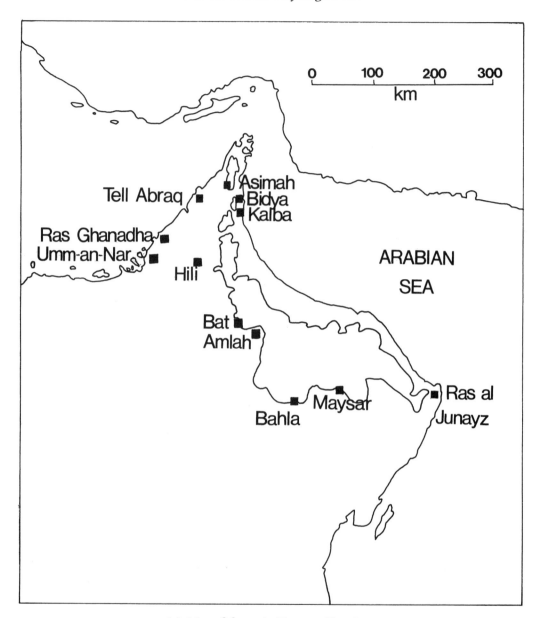

6.1 Map of the main Umm-an-Nar sites.

that, as in the case of the rest of Arabia, these subsistence strategies were in many cases complementary and that the same group of people made use of several types of resource. There is archaeological evidence for human exploitation of the coastal region from the late Palaeolithic (e.g. de Cardi 1978) although little can be said about their way of life in which fishing played an important part. From the late fourth millennium there are a few indications of settlement found below better preserved later sites at Hili and Bat for example. The appearance of stone-built tombs at about this time does not of itself necessarily indicate permanent settlement, because nomadic peoples are known to construct elaborate graves,[17] but their presence does suggest an increasingly prosperous and sophisticated population. Common sense and ethnography allow us to propose that both settled and nomadic elements were present, although this cannot be demonstrated from the archaeological evidence. If this proposition is accepted, it would seem likely that close relations existed between the two groups as we have already seen was the case in Eastern Arabia.

It is possible to draw immediate contrasts between the economy of the coastal sites such as Tell Abraq, Umm-an-Nar and Ras Ghanadha, with their heavy reliance on the sea, and the inland oasis sites like Hili, Bat and Maysar where irrigation agriculture was practised and copper-working played an important economic role. At Umm-an-Nar a large amount of fishbone from a wide range of species was found as well as the remains of sea mammals like turtles and dugong. The bulk of the protein eaten on the island seems to have come from the sea. Bird bones included those of the now extinct giant heron and peregrine falcons. Sheep, goat and camel bone were also found, together with a few pieces of dog. It was not possible from the small sample to determine whether the camel was domesticated. The bones from Ras Ghanadha indicate the importance of dugong in the diet (Hoch 1979; al-Tikriti 1985: 17 n.12). It is interesting in this context to note that the human teeth from Umm-an-Nar suggested that cereals were not an important part of the diet in these coastal sites. At Abraq, where analyses are still in progress, marine resources were also important, but domesticated animals seem to have played a more important role than at the other two sites discussed above (Potts 1993a).

Inland the situation was very different. Here each site had its own agricultural resources, and there is direct evidence for simple irrigation techniques such as gabar-bands to trap the water and the silt as they ran down off the mountains (Hastings *et al*. 1975). The indirect evidence from the botanical remains also indicates irrigation. Dates were found at Hili and at Maysar where the remains of matting shows that the leaves were also being used, perhaps indicating local production (Weisgerber 1980: 105). Remains of melon seeds from Hili suggest that fruit was being grown in the shade of the palm trees as is still the practice today (Cleuziou 1989: 79), while cereal remains from this site include three types of cultivated barley, two types of wheat, and wild oats, which probably grew as a weed on the fringes of the cultivated areas. At Bat, Brunswick found traces of terraced gardens which he suggested might have been used for the cultivation of dates (Brunswick 1989: 19).

Sheep and goat were extensively herded throughout the area and cattle were also

---

[17] The magnificent graves found in the permafrost at Pazyrak for example are attributed to nomadic hordes.

present. The remains from Hili suggest that they may have been used for traction, but other draft animals were also known as the skeleton of a donkey was found close to the well in Maysar 25 (Weisgerber 1981: 249), and camel bones were identified from Abraq, as well as from Umm-an-Nar where they were used for the manufacture of spindle whorls (Frifelt 1995: 222). The evidence for the probable local domestication of the camel by the middle of the third millennium is of considerable importance, particularly in terms of the potential they offered as a means of transport. The bones of wild animals, which include large mammals like gazelle, and small ones like hares, were found on both coastal and inland sites and no doubt provided a welcome additional source of protein.

THE ARCHAEOLOGICAL EVIDENCE

The earliest evidence for human activity in the area comes from scattered evidence for aceramic flint-working sites in the Oman peninsula (e.g. cf. Inizan 1988; Weisgerber 1981: 254). Some of the earliest ceramic sites have already been mentioned in chapter 2; Ubaid pottery was found at the shell-midden site 69 in Umm-al-Qawain (Boucharlat *et al.* 1991), in Ajman (Haerinck 1994), and in a group of burials at Site 2 close to Tell Abraq. The flint work from these burials is similar to that from another group of graves (Phillips pers. comm.), this time without stratified pottery, found at RH5 on the Indian Ocean (Coppa *et al.* 1985). The two groups of burials may well be contemporary. In addition, the survey of Ras Abaruk by de Cardi and her team in 1973 identified pottery of all types from Ubaid 2 to Ubaid 5, accompanied by a coarser, apparently locally-made ware (de Cardi 1978). More recently important sites have been found on a number of offshore islands, most notably Dalma (see chapter 2). As archaeological activity intensifies, more and more coastal sites with Ubaid pottery are being identified. The distribution of the majority of sites along the ancient shoreline points to the importance of fishing in the economy and to marine-based contacts with the Ubaid homeland in Mesopotamia. The situation seems to be similar to that in Eastern Arabia (see chapter 2), although there is no evidence in the Oman peninsula for the dissemination of the pottery inland.

The first substantial structures in the Oman peninsula are, perhaps, a thousand years later in date than the latest Ubaid pottery. Large numbers of stone-built graves are found prominently sited on the rocky ridges of the al Hajar range (Fig. 6.2), while others of a rather different configuration are found on lower ground. They are found from the Umm-an-Nar area to the al Hajar mountains and down to the Sharqiyah. The tombs can be divided into two types. Both are stone-built, the first group is conical and in shape they apparently resemble an old fashioned thimble, though no evidence for their original roofing survives; this type of grave is usually constructed with a number of concentric ring walls in the interior around the actual burial chamber, the

6.2 'Thimble' graves.

space between being filled with smaller stones. The entrance is through a well-defined door and entrance passage which leads to the centrally-placed chamber. Tombs of this type are often placed on elevated ridges and because of their high visibility have been extensively robbed so that little direct evidence remains for their dating. They were used for two millennia and similar ones were constructed in the Iron Age. However, Vogt has presented a case on stylistic grounds for the early examples being partly contemporary with the second type of grave, known as Hafit, which can be dated to the late fourth or early third millennium (Vogt 1985). This second type of tomb has a lower, humped profile; it is usually built of an inner and an outer wall only, the space between the two being filled with rubble and the whole construction covered with a mound of stones. The entrance is not well-defined and cannot always be identified. Where the evidence is available, it seems that in both types of grave the tomb chamber was originally corbel vaulted and there is space only for three or four burials, so they cannot be seen as true collective graves.

A number of the Hafit type graves have now been excavated and jars comparable in shape and fabric to examples dating to the Mesopotamian Jemdat Nasr/Early Dynastic I/II periods, about 3100–2700 BC, have been found in them (Frifelt 1975a, 1980; Potts 1986a). The jars are biconical with a short neck and everted rim and typically are covered in a plum-coloured wash, sometimes decorated on the upper part of the body with designs in black on a white ground (see Fig. 2.6). The paint is fugitive and rubs off very easily so that the jars are often found with no trace of paint surviving. The shape, however, is very distinctive. Scraps of copper and simple implements were also recovered from the graves together with beads of many different materials including carnelian. Frifelt attempted to link some of these artefacts with Mesopotamian proto-types, but the forms are so simple that the exercise lacks rigour (Frifelt 1980: 275). In addition, at least one tomb of this date, Cairn 4 at Tawi Silaim, produced faience beads (de Cardi *et al.* 1979). This material, which can only be made with quite a high level of technical competence, is found in Mesopotamia from the late Ubaid period and its use becomes more widespread from the late fourth millennium onwards (Moorey 1985: 142–5). The technology may well, however, have been locally available, as the scraps of copper in the tombs and the distribution of the graves close to the copper sources both indicate some knowledge of pyrotechnology.

Few of the Hafit graves are found in direct association with settlements, although the majority seem to relate to the major east/west and north/south routes outlined above and they are often distributed close to the major mining areas (Potts 1981). Exceptionally, at Maysar 25 there is also a close relationship between the tower-like round enclosure and two Hafit graves containing Jemdat Nasr type pottery which lie inside the walls (Weisgerber 1981: 199). The excavator states that the graves predate the walls of the tower. The area of Maysar in the Wadi Samad is rich in copper and the presence of numerous Hafit graves, in addition to the two mentioned above, close to an area of mining known as Maysar 2, suggests strongly that copper was already being extracted and was playing an important part in the economy of the area by the late fourth millennium. More generally, Cleuziou and Tosi have suggested that Hafit graves are broadly contemporary with the earliest phase of the round, fortified structure at Hili 8 which will be described later (Cleuziou and Tosi 1989: 19).

In view of the concentration of Hafit graves along the routes to the mines and in the areas around them, it seems plausible to link the presence of Jemdat Nasr pottery in some of the Hafit graves with the extraction of copper. The breakdown in the late Uruk trading network linking Mesopotamia with the copper resources of south-east Anatolia makes the theory all the more attractive (Algaze 1993). We can suggest that Mesopotamia had to look elsewhere for its metal and its timber and turned southwards to re-establish old connections. Many questions remain unanswered and proof of direct contact between Mesopotamia and Oman is still missing. We do not know how or where the copper was exchanged. We do not even know if the exchanges were made directly between people from the mines and Mesopotamian 'buyers', or through middlemen.

What we do know of this early period indicates that a highly organized and central-ized system is unlikely as the administrative infrastructure did not exist in the Oman peninsula, although it was beginning to develop in south Mesopotamia (Nissen 1993). The virtual absence of Jemdat Nasr pottery in Bahrain and the Eastern Province would suggest direct contact between Mesopotamia and what is today the United Arab Emirates, the area where such pottery occurs in some quantity, but there is still no evidence that people from Mesopotamia travelled inland to the mines. If they had, one might expect the occasional 'foreign' burial at the mine sites[18] and the distribution of the imported pottery would probably cluster round the mines where their business would have been transacted. Instead, the pottery is spread out along the major arteries of communication (Gentelle and Frifelt 1989), a pattern of distribution which is often taken to indicate a down-the-line type of trading contact (Renfrew and Bahn 1991). On the evidence we have at present it seems probable that ships from Mesopotamia docked at coastal sites like Umm-an-Nar which gave easy access to the route to Buraimi and south to Maysar and other mining sites. Here they acquired the precious copper in return for whatever was contained in the painted jars. Beads and perishable goods like foodstuffs and textiles may also have been offered in exchange to the miners or their agents. Some of these goods then trickled down to the people who lived along the route between the port and the mines, as gifts, 'taxes', or to smooth the passage of the caravans travelling between the mines and the coast. Being highly prized, the pots were sometimes deposited as grave goods. Alternatively, ships from Oman may also have travelled to ports like Ur in south Mesopotamia, returning loaded with jars and other Mesopotamian produce.

THE THIRD MILLENNIUM: SETTLEMENT AND ARCHITECTURE

Apart from the graves and the limited range of artefacts preserved in them, we have no information on how these earliest copper miners lived. It is only in the early third millennium, in the period called after the coastal site of Umm-an-Nar, which follows on from that in which the Jemdat Nasr pottery occurs, that we can begin to reconstruct something of their way of life. Recently Orchard and Stranger (1994) have suggested that at this time the Oman peninsula was home to not one, but two, closely related material cultures, the largely coastal Umm-an-Nar and the oasis al Hajar culture. This suggestion remains to be fully developed, but both the architectural and the funerary evidence would point to considerable coherence throughout the region, although regional differences can be seen in the pottery corpus. In this chapter the evidence will be treated as representing a single Umm-an-Nar culture.

A number of settlements of this date are known, most of which lie close to sources of copper and many of which are distinguished by the presence of one or more tower-like

---

[18] Frifelt (1980: 278) has suggested that some of the Hafit graves which contain objects of possible Mesopotamian manufacture may be those of 'Sumerian' merchants.

buildings. The distribution of these towers runs from the Arabian Gulf to the Indian Ocean and from the area of Sharjar to the Sharqiyah. The best known are at the site of Hili close to al Ain, excavated by French and Danish archaeologists over a number of years and providing a sequence of deposits which cover the whole of the third millennium, even spilling over into the second. There were at least four towers at Hili 1, 4 and 8, and 11 (Orchard 1994). Other important sites are known at Bat, where six towers and associated houses were identified (Frifelt 1976). Smaller concentrations have been found at a large number of sites which, moving roughly north to south include: Tell Abraq, partially excavated by Dan Potts (Potts 1993b); Bidya on the Indian Ocean where two towers were identified and one has been excavated (al Tikriti 1989); west of Bat at Khutm and at Dariz at least three more towers were identified by survey but no details are available (Gentelle and Frifelt 1989: 123). Others have been located in the Wadi Bahla (Orchard and Stranger 1994), near Amlah (de Cardi *et al.* 1976; Hastings *et al.* 1975: 12–13; Humphries 1974), at Maysar and nearby at al Khasbah (Weisgerber 1980: 99–100). At most of the excavated sites, except perhaps Bidya, copper-working or smelting has been identified.

These tower houses are built of brick, stone or a combination of both, usually on a raised foundation. The material used seems to have depended on the local availability of stone. Some have additional perimeter walls or ditches, some have clearly defined internal walls, others appear to have had none. They are often associated with stone-built wells either within the perimeter wall or close beside it. The combination of strong walls, ditches and a safe water supply suggests that some at least of them had defensive functions, as do the traditional towers still found in much of the area today (Fig. 6.3) (see for instance Kennet's 1995 survey of the towers of Ras al Khaimah) (Connolly 1995). The smallest examples were probably watch towers like the two in the Wadi Bahla described by Orchard, each just over six metres in diameter (Orchard and Stranger 1994: 78).

The suggestion of defensive function is strengthened by the observation that in a number of cases the towers are placed in pairs on either side of a wadi or track in such a way that it appears that an approaching enemy could be caught in a pincer movement between them. This positioning can be seen at Bidya where Bidya 2 and 4 are on opposite sides of the wadi leading from the mountains to the coastal plain (Fig. 6.4); at al Khasbar where survey work identified two towers in the same relative position (Weisgerber 1980: 99); possibly in the Wadi Bahla at sites 37.i & ii, (de Cardi, Collier and Bell 1976: 163) and at Bat where Frifelt's 1976 map shows three towers clustered on either side of the present day wadi (1976: 63). If these observations are valid, and further excavation is needed to show the contemporaneity of the pairs of buildings identified by survey, it suggests that attacks were a common occurrence throughout much of the third millennium and beyond and that the small communities were coordinated against them.

6.3 Modern tower at Jazirat al Hamra.

It is now generally accepted that the architecture of any society does to some extent mirror the values and needs of that society, as well as playing an active role in promoting socially desirable behaviour (Hillier and Penn 1991; Kent 1990). This means that we may tentatively use the architectural remains of past societies to model their social organization, together with evidence drawn from the finds and from ethnography where this is available. The architecture of the tower houses, some of which as we shall see, stand amongst other flimsier houses, suggests a society with some degree of social differentiation and a need for protection. The towers at Bat, Hili and Maysar are all associated with the remains of much less impressive domestic and industrial buildings, which cluster around the protecting towers. In Arabia the ethnographic analogy provided by the defensive towers of today, which belong mainly to the shaikhly families and also stand amongst unfortified houses, suggests that the third-millennium society was in some respects similar.

These analogies are merely pointers; there is little other evidence for a stratified society in the third millennium and other interpretations for the ancient towers could be suggested. They might, for instance, have been places of refuge for the whole community, rather than status dwellings for a few richer families. There is little archaeological evidence for their use in either capacity because of poor preservation which has in most cases destroyed the floor levels so that the associated small finds have also eroded away. However, the differences in construction and plan which can still be

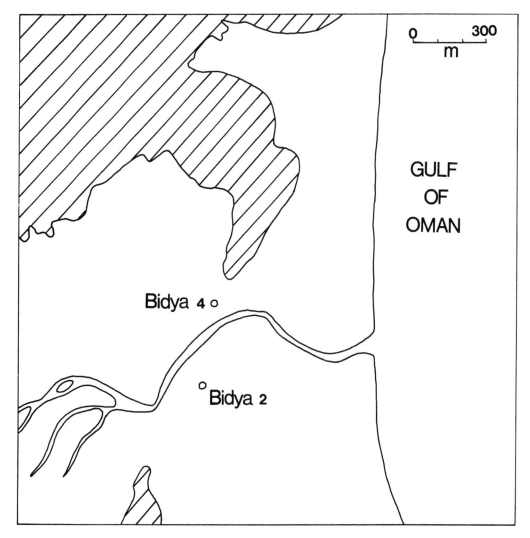

6.4 Plan of Bidya to show positions of towers at the mouth of the wadi.

observed indicate that not all of them necessarily served the same function. Some with wells and fireplaces seem to have been habitations, while those with no internal constructions, such as BB19, which is forty metres in diameter with no visible internal walls, may have served another purpose (Humphries 1974: 60. Note: this may be the same site as de Cardi *et al.* 1976: 163 37.iii). It is difficult to see how this structure could have been roofed, though it may, like Maysar, have had rooms built around the perimeter. Perhaps this type of tower acted as a corral or compound in which stock, too, could be protected from raiders. We will look first at those towers which were apparently largely roofed, and then at the others.

6.5 The stepped outer wall of a tower house at Bat.

The towers at Hili 8 (Cleuziou 1989) and Bat (Frifelt 1976; Brunswick 1989) are the most fully published and offer a number of interesting contrasts, although these are obviously outweighed by the similarities between them. As we have already seen, each stood in irrigable areas, between the mountains and the desert, amongst other buildings which are poorly preserved. Other towers have been identified in the immediate neighbourhood of each (see p. 112). At Bat it has been estimated that the inhabited area covered as much as forty to fifty hectares (Frifelt 1976: 60). Each tower is raised on a platform to enhance its safety and has a well in the centre of the building. The tower at Hili 8 is sub-circular and about seventeen metres in diameter, built entirely of mud-brick, while the Bat example is about twenty metres across with a stepped external ring wall of stone blocks (Fig. 6.5), apparently approached by a ramp or steps on the south (Frifelt 1976). Additional rooms abut the external wall on the north-east. Inside the ring wall three rooms were excavated to give a cross section of the building and it was shown that the internal walls were standing to a height of two and a half metres in some cases, but were not bonded with the exterior wall. It seems likely, on analogy with the more recent excavations at Hili, that the excavated walls formed a sub-structure, rather than internal rooms, as no associated floors are reported. On the other hand, the building is heavily eroded and the floors may have been lost. A fireplace was found below the level of the walls which relates to the construction phase of the building, another feature which can be paralleled at Hili. The wellhead is finely made of carefully shaped blocks of stone, but its height relative to the partition walls is not given so it cannot be used to determine the original floor levels.

The tower at Hili 8 (Cleuziou 1989) had three major phases of construction of which the first, phase I, is the best preserved. It is built of flat mudbricks on virgin soil and, as at Bat, the internal walls do not key into the outer sub-circular wall and form a substructure filled with sand and gravel for the living area above. The interior of this platform is divided symetrically into rows of rectangular chambers on either side of a central well. The well is a sophisticated structure with a square chamber four metres below the surface and a shaft, square at the base and round at the top. The top section is stone-lined. The C14 dates from hearths associated with the construction phase of the tower give dates in the region of 2450±100 BC uncalibrated, so the building would seem to date back to the early third millennium. There is evidence for an additional rectangular platform on the east side of the tower which was subdivided into three with a flat plaster surface on which could be seen the impressions of cereal grains. Three ditches, which may have been defensive, one of which underlies the additional platform, and so predates it, were traced around part of the tower. On the other hand, it is also possible that they may be connected with the irrigation of the gardens which seem to have surrounded the tower. Irrigation lay at the basis of the community's prosperity and its infrastructure was well worth defending.

The second phase of the Hili 8 building is still associated with the Umm-an-Nar period, which is thought to cover most of the third millennium. The outer wall was completely reshaped as a true circle using plano-convex bricks which have a superficial similarity to those from Early Dynastic Mesopotamia, but which are considerably larger and which are not laid in the herring-bone fashion typical of Mesopotamia. Two or more ditches again surround the complex. A new well was sunk outside the perimeter wall but within the platform mentioned before lying on the east side of the building. This well is eight and a half metres deep, suggesting a drop in the water table from phase I, when the well was only four metres in depth. The new well continued in use into phase III. No trace of internal rooms was recovered from this period, but once again other rooms were identified between the tower and the surrounding ditches. In the last phase of this building, phase IIe, evidence for copper-working and other craft activities was recovered from a terrace east of the tower. Copper seems to have been alloyed with tin and percentages of up to 5 per cent are found. The origin of the tin is still unknown, but it may have originated in Afghanistan. The hearths associated with the metal-working area have provided calibrated C14 dates of 2470±150 and 2400±150 BC (Cleuziou 1989).

The tower was rebuilt for a third time in phase IIf and the external wall moved eastwards to include the well of period 2. There are still no internal walls, but once again, a number of rooms were identified east of the tower, one of which contained three steps of a stair. The C14 dates from this phase cluster around 2200 BC calibrated.

The final phase of the tower, period III, is marked by the introduction of a new style of pottery and a new construction technique. It is not clear if this phase follows on directly from the final Umm-an-Nar phase or if there was a period of abandonment: if there was it must have been a short one to judge from the C14 dates and the re-use of the external wall of the tower built in phase IIf. New architectural features are found abutting it in period III. These are badly damaged, but seem to consist of a circular enclosure wall, the lower parts of which are built of stone for the first time (Cleuziou 1981: 280 Fig. 2 for plan). They are built of an inner and an outer face of slabs with a filling of small stones between, possibly capped by further stone slabs, a technique which can also be seen in the contemporary tombs. Traces of interior walls, and of floors were recovered, but the level was badly eroded and no plans could be reconstructed. A C14 date places these walls in the Wadi Suq period of the early second millennium. The site is then abandoned until the Iron Age when it was probably used as a burial ground.

In view of the lack of internal features in the two later tower buildings it should perhaps be asked whether the function of the building changed during its history. In the earliest phase it seems to have been a dwelling, but in period II it may have become a corral and place of safety with the living accommodation represented by the additional buildings between the tower and the ditches. On the other hand, the lack of internal features may be illusory and the result of severe erosion rather than of change of usage. The tower excavated by Frifelt at Hili I (Frifelt 1975b: 370), which has no overburden, and so could be expected to have suffered from even more severe natural processes of erosion, still retains its internal walls which show a marked similarity to those of the earliest phase of Hili 8. This observation would tend to support the suggestion that the phase II building at Hili never had internal walls.

The badly eroded tower at Bidya 2 on the Indian Ocean, with a diameter of twenty-six metres, has traces of both internal walls and buildings abutting it, though there is no firm evidence for a well within the perimeter. It may have lain adjacent to the tower below a well which is still in use (al Tikriti 1989a). What appears to be a tower similar to Hili 8 was identified by survey near Amlah, south of Bat, where Site 41.11 consisted of a circular building about ten metres in diameter with a number of rectangular structures abutting it on the south. There is some evidence for other smaller tower buildings at nearby Site 3, a situation which is paralleled at the so-called 'town' at Bat (de Cardi *et al.* 1976).

The question of the internal arrangements of these towers has also to be asked about the very large tower at Tell Abraq on the Gulf of Oman which has a diameter of forty metres and, like Bidya, has a stone perimeter wall and mudbrick internal walls. However, it seems to belong to our second type with largely unroofed interiors. Its diameter is comparable to that of the unexcavated BB19 and a test trench through the centre of the Abraq tower suggests that this was an open courtyard area, perhaps with rooms around the perimeter of the building. A modern parallel can be seen in the magnificent and well-known tower at Nizwa (Rice 1994). Like Hili 8, Abraq continued in use after the end of the Umm-an-Nar period and owes its exceptional preservation to the fact that it was enclosed below a heavy mudbrick platform of late second-millennium date (Potts 1993a: 118).

Yet another tower, which may relate morphologically to that at Abraq, as it too has an open courtyard with rooms round the perimeter, has been excavated in the Wadi Samad. Maysar 25 forms part of an important group of archaeological remains. These sites are related, as we have already seen, to the adjacent copper resources which were exploited from the early third millennium at least until the third quarter of the second. The earliest remains are the Hafit type graves from Maysar 3 which have already been mentioned. Most lie on the flanks of the mountains, but two lie within and below a circular building known as Maysar 25 (Weisgerber 1981: 198). Like the Bat and the Hili towers it stands on a raised foundation and has a stone-built circular perimeter wall with an external diameter of 21.60 m. Inside the wall are two rooms against one arc of the wall, one of which contains the bottom steps of a stair. A third room was identified on the opposite side of the enclosure and a large well in the centre. No fireplaces were identified within the building (Weisgerber 1981: 203) which may suggest that here we are looking at a temporary refuge for men and animals, rather than at a permanent dwelling. The two graves below the building may have had some special significance for the people of Maysar and so have been judged worthy of special protection. An alternative interpretation might suggest that the tower served a ritual purpose connected with the presence of the graves. If this is the case, the building is unique in the Oman peninsula at this period.

Orchard has pointed out the presence of a group of impressive tiered structures usually built round the top of a rocky outcrop, some of which seem to be contemporary with the tower houses. She suggests that these may have served a ceremonial or other public function. Most of those identified lie in and around the Wadi Bahla, which has been extensively surveyed, though one, at an-Nabaghiya, lies four kilometres from Bat and is made up of three terraces, the top one being about 22 × 18 m in size. Orchard suggests it marked one of the boundaries of the ancient settlement at Bat, but its date is unclear (Orchard and Stranger 1994: 72). Orchard also describes three examples from the Bisya area, two of which seem to be third-millennium in date and all of which are formed of terraces around an outcrop. It has been suggested that they may have supported civic or public buildings of some kind (Orchard and Stranger 1994: 73), but only at Qarn Qarhat la Hwid have structures survived and their nature is unclear, though two or three retaining walls were identified and graves were also present (for a plan see Humphries 1974: 60 Fig. 3).

6.6 Maysar, view of houses.

Rectilinear architecture is relatively poorly represented in the Oman peninsula during the third millennium and Maysar (Fig. 6.6) is one of the few sites to have given us evidence for buildings of an entirely different sort which seem to be, at least in part, contemporary with the towers, though they continue in use into the Wadi Suq period after most of the towers go out of use. Survey at Maysar has identified a settlement at Maysar 1 which the excavator dates to the late third/early second millennium; it has a number of rectangular houses, two of which appear to have smaller rooms in one corner, a plan which is also found at a similar period at Saar, Bahrain (Weisgerber 1980 abb.28: 78). Unfortunately the detailed plans have not yet been published. Such results as are available show that copper-working took place within the houses; a stock of bun-shaped ingots was found in House 4, an anvil and hammerstones in House 6, another metal-working area lay below House 31 and the northern area of the site is described by the excavator as a workman's quarter where there is also evidence for the manufacture of steatite/chlorite vessels decorated with the dot and circle motifs typical of the *série tardive* group of vessels (Weisgerber 1981: 78).

Evidence for manufacturing activity has also been found on the coast at Tell Abraq and at the island of Umm-an-Nar. At Abraq the tower house is associated with what are probably fragments of furnace linings with droplets of copper on them and a copper ingot (Potts 1993a). Umm-an-Nar island seems to have been an important stop-over on the route from Mesopotamia to the copper mines of Oman and a settlement, a metal-working area with extensive burning and scraps of melted and smelted copper, and a number of fine graves have been found, all dating to the third millennium. This settlement has no towers, but the incomplete remains of a number of stone-built 'houses' were recovered by successive expeditions. In addition, a workshop or ware-house made up of seven long, narrow, magazine-type rooms and covering an area of c. 300 square metres has been uncovered (Frifelt 1995). The excavator suggested that the upper part of the walls may have been of perishable materials because of the relatively limited amount of stone debris. Sadly, none of the plans is complete, but there is no evidence in the excavated portions of the large building for fireplaces or other domestic installations. This, and the large numbers of tools, support the idea that the building is a workshop or a magazine. Three phases were identified all of which seem to date to the third millennium to judge from the pottery found within them (cf. also al Tikriti 1981). This date is also supported by a single seal impression on a potsherd which Amiet has now dated to the middle of the third millennium on the basis of comparisons with Syrian material (Amiet 1986: 172).

No exactly comparable buildings are known on the Arabian mainland, but a number of rectilinear domestic buildings are known throughout the region; a much smaller building of similar date with two rectangular rooms was recently excavated at Asimah 99 (Vogt 1994: 152) and at Zahra 1, close to the eastern end of the Wadi Jizzi, two small copper-working settlements were identified, each with rectilinear houses (Costa and Wilkinson 1987). We have already seen some slight evidence for rectilinear domestic architecture in the Eastern Province at Umm-an-Nussi and Tell ar-Ramadh (see chapter 3). In addition, there are the remains of flimsier structures associated with the tower houses at both Bat and Tell Abraq and it has been suggested that these represent summer houses of palm leaves of the type in use throughout the Gulf region until modern times (Fig. 6.7). Similar temporary buildings may have been present at Ras Ghanada, a site east of Umm-an-Nar which probably had a similar function as a trading post, but where no building remains were recovered (al Tikriti 1985). The evidence from these sites confirms the presence of a variety of forms of architecture throughout the third and early second millennia. The tower houses are only the most impressive manifestation of this architectural diversity to have survived. It is somewhat surprising that, unless Orchard is right in her interpretation of the 'tiered structures', no public buildings of any kind are known. (It is arguable that the 'tiered structures' are in fact defensible retreats rather than public buildings.) There are no firmly identified religious buildings, and no palaces or administrative buildings, although the technical competence to build them clearly existed. This seems to indicate a dispersed, loosely structured social system where such buildings were not required and in which small groups of buildings clustered round one or more tower houses in pockets of irrigated land. A number of such nuclei can be seen in relatively close proximity within the oases at sites like Bat or Hili, but cannot be seen as forming urban conglomerations (*contra* Orchard 1994). They lack the evidence for specialization, stratification and administrative devices essential for the recognition of a town.

6.7 Barasti or palm leaf hut.

THE EARLY SECOND MILLENNIUM

In the succeeding Wadi Suq period there seems to have been considerable discontinuity in the settlement pattern and the evidence for permanent occupation is much reduced (Fig. 6.8). The reasons for this dislocation seem likely to be connected with progressive dessication in the region, with the transfer of the focus of the copper trade to Dilmun at the end of the Ur III period *c.* 2000 BC and with changes in the relationship with the great Harappan cities of the Indus. These events must have had immediate economic consequences for the people of Magan, but did not spell economic ruin; the settlement at Umm-an-Nar was deserted, but Abraq continued to flourish and it seems likely that there are substantial buildings of early second-millennium date at Nud Ziba and Bidaʿa (Carter forthcoming). There is also some limited evidence for stone-built rectilinear structures at Shimal, as well as for lighter temporary buildings. Further south, the village at Maysar continued to produce chlorite vessels, and it has been suggested that a complex of mudbrick platforms and walls at Tawi Said may date to this period, but no pottery of the Wadi Suq period was found in direct association with the walls (de Cardi *et al.* 1979). Other sites of the early second millennium will undoubtedly be found when the fertile Batinah coast is more thoroughly explored, but intense agricultural activity in this area makes the identification of archaeological sites very difficult, even when they have survived repeated cycles of cultivation. For example, an impressive tower of second- and third-millennium date has recently been identified at Kalba in the northern Batinah by Carl Phillips of the Institute of Archaeology, University College, London.

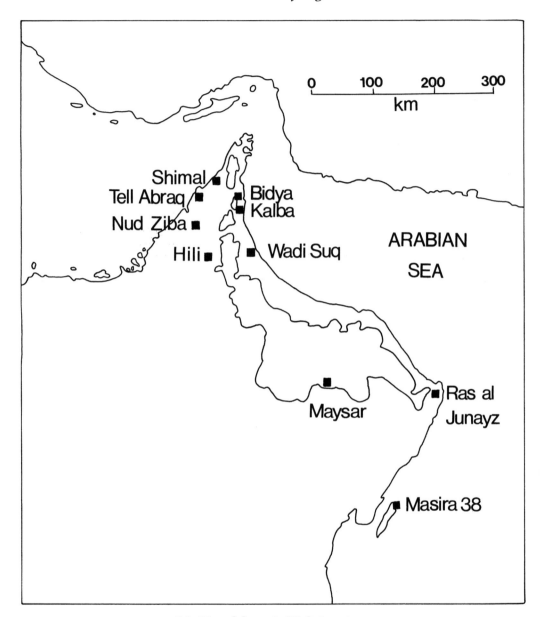

6.8 Map of the main Wadi Suq sites.

Ras al Junayz in the south-east of the Arabian Peninsula becomes of increasing importance about this time and perhaps takes over some of the functions of Ras al Hadd slightly further north, which seems to have been a major point of contact with the Indus valley in the third millennium. At Ras al Junayz, one of the sites excavated yielded part of a mudbrick magazine containing slabs of bitumen, apparently for trade with the Indus. This site also yielded a sherd scratched with four Harappan signs and seals with Indus valley signs on them, as well as two seals which may perhaps show signs belonging to a local script (Cleuziou *et al.* 1994; Tosi 1986: 106).

SUMMARY

There is then, incontrovertible evidence for permanent settlement throughout the third and early second millennia in all parts of the Oman peninsula, even though there is a marked decline in the amount of evidence around 2000 BC. The distribution of the settlements indicates a range of subsistence strategies, while the nature of the buildings suggests a society that was already, to some extent, socially differentiated and which was accustomed to defending itself. The apparent absence of public buildings suggests that society was organized in small groups with no overarching political structure. On the other hand, the uniformity observed in many aspects of the material culture throughout the area indicates close contacts of some kind, and the network of commercial ties linking groups with complementary economic strategies probably explains the regularities. The absence of any religious buildings is surprising as the care and effort invested in the burials of the time strongly suggests a belief in an afterlife. Further evidence for the organization of society can be seen in these tombs and will be described in the next chapter.

Chapter 7

THE OMAN PENINSULA: GRAVES AND ARTEFACTS

It is now generally accepted that burials are one of the most useful tools an archaeologist has for reconstructing an ancient society, although the relationship between the dead and the living is not a simple one. The method of burial and the nature of the grave goods may directly reflect the life lived by the deceased and their position in the social hierarchy; it may represent an idealized position rather than a real one, or it may be conditioned by religious beliefs which dictate a particular method of disposal on purely ideological grounds as with Islam or Christianity (Morris 1992). In the absence of any evidence to the contrary, the burials of the Oman peninsula are assumed to fall into the first category and to reflect the social systems of the time. As on Bahrain, the range of rites for which we have evidence suggests a society composed of a number of different groups, each with their own distinctive customs; this would match the evidence for the range of economic and subsistence strategies on the peninsula which also suggest different groups within the community. It could be argued that the different rites found were seen as appropriate for different classes of individuals within a single group, but there is no evidence to support this. The skeletal evidence shows that the predominant rite for both sexes, and apparently for all ages, for most of the third millennium, was multiple burial in fine stone-built tombs. Some instances of cremation and single inhumation are also known. The building skills of the architects of the Umm-an-Nar period discussed in the last chapter, are again demonstrated by these free-standing, circular monuments which are found throughout much of Oman and the UAE. The finds from the tombs offer some of the best evidence we have for the technological expertise of the people buried in them as well as offering clues about their social organization. Forty-nine of these tombs were identified on Umm-an-Nar island itself and will be discussed first (Frifelt 1991).

The tombs on the island vary in size from 18 m in diameter to 1.75 m, but most have features in common. They are built free-standing, frequently on a plinth, with a double ring wall, the outer face of which is usually formed of finely cut, beautifully finished *ashlar* blocks or slabs. Some of these blocks can be ornamented with human or animal figures in relief. Some of the finest examples of these decorated slabs come from al Ain where a tomb from Hili has been reconstructed in a public park (Fig. 7.1). It is decorated with a variety of human and animal figures (Fig. 7.2). From Grave II on Umm-an-Nar island come slabs depicting a bull and camels as well as what the excavator describes as an idol, a schematic human figure.

124

7.1 The reconstructed tomb from Hili grave in the al Ain archaeological park.

7.2 Animal figures on an Umm-an-Nar grave.

7.3 Plan of an Umm-an-Nar grave at Shimal.

Except in the smallest examples, the interior of the graves is divided in plan into a minimum of two chambers, sometimes with a passage between them (Fig. 7.3). Sometimes they are also divided horizontally into two levels. The chambers appear to have been corbel vaulted and sometimes have stone-paved floors. They house multiple burials and analysis of the human remains has suggested that the graves at Umm-an-Nar contain members of family groups. However, women and children seem to be under-represented in these graves which might support the suggestion made by a number of scholars that this settlement was a specialist centre for traders and sailors, rather than an ordinary community with the standard distribution of ages and sexes (Frifelt 1991: 125 and chapter 4: 12). It might, on the other hand, merely mean that a different burial rite was employed for some members of the group. Some evidence certainly exists for a second rite as a number of extramural burials are noted associated with some of the cairns, notably outside Grave V, and cremations were also reported, but there is no osteological evidence to link these other rites into single categories by age or sex. A study of the teeth from the tombs, which do not show the signs of heavy wear usually associated with coarsely ground flour, suggests that cereals did not play a significant part in the diet of the people of the island, an interesting finding in view of the paucity of palaeobotanical evidence for the presence of wheat or barley at this time.

7.4 Umm-an-Nar pottery in the al Ain museum.

The entrance to the tombs is often closed with a specially tailored stone which sometimes has a lug handle, as in Grave I, to facilitate the reopening of the tomb to allow further interments. If necessary, earlier burials were pushed to one side, or piled in a heap to make room for the new body. The grave goods are very varied and include weapons, tools, beads, stone vessels and a wide variety of pottery. One cylindrical bowl of dark green steatite which probably belongs to the Intercultural group of stone vessels was found in Grave 1 (Frifelt 1991: 105 Fig. 220), while another sherd with a fragmentary Hut pot pattern was found in the settlement (Frifelt 1995a: 198) and is at present the most southerly occurrence of this distinctive type yet found (see chapter 3).

The pottery corpus includes fine black on grey and incised vessels which appear to be Iranian in origin as well as plain buff ware pots from Mesopotamia (Fig. 7.4). Both imported and local wares also link the island with inland sites like Hili (see pp. 115–17). The jewellery, too, has foreign elements and includes beads made of lapis lazuli and of etched carnelian, the latter originating in the Indus valley (Frifelt 1991: 116). Traces of the flax used to twist the string on which the beads were strung have also been recovered. Finds like the imported pottery and the beads underline again the far-reaching connections of the site throughout the third millennium.

These Umm-an-Nar tombs, as the type is called, are found widely distributed in the UAE and Oman. Two especially fine examples were excavated at Hili, one, mentioned above, has now been rebuilt in a public garden in al Ain.[19] The other, Tomb A, has a

---

[19] Other tombs from Hili include Tomb M which was badly destroyed, and Tomb B, both of which date to the earlier part of the Umm-an-Nar sequence (Cleuziou 1989).

diameter of ten and a half metres and had two storeys separated by a stone floor, the
lower one being sunk one and a half metres into the ground (Vogt 1985a). It is estimated that about ninety people were buried here and the range of grave goods is similar
to that from Umm-an-Nar. Instead of the links with Mesopotamia, however, there are
a greater number of sherds and etched carnelian beads which originated in the Indus
valley. There is some Iranian material as at Umm-an-Nar island and one wheel-turned,
softstone flask has been identified as Bactrian. The pottery indicates a date towards the
end of the Umm-an-Nar period, when contacts with the Indus valley increase in importance, apparently at the expense of those with Mesopotamia, which in any case were
never close at inland sites. It may be asked why a site like Hili should have so many
imported goods from such far flung places and we can only suggest that it reflects the
great wealth or importance of the site.

Another Umm-an-Nar grave of third-millennium date comes from Tell Abraq, where
it is closely associated with the tower house, underlying an early stage of the outer wall
of the building. The grave is only six metres in diameter, but is estimated to have contained a minimum of 155 individuals. In contrast to the tombs on Umm-an-Nar island,
it has been suggested that 'the tomb was used by individuals originating in more than
one population' perhaps reflecting the mixed nature of the inhabitants of this seaport
(Potts 1993b: 121 quoting Wright). Like the Hili A tomb the Abraq tomb seems to date
from the end of the Umm-an-Nar period and a C14 date of 2190–30 was obtained from
a level immediately predating its construction. There is slight evidence at this site, as
there is from other contemporary graves, for an area outside the grave where some kind
of rituals could have taken place. In the case of Abraq the pavement below the burial
chambers extends beyond the grave to the south and its southern perimeter is marked
by several upright stone slabs and a threshold (Potts 1993b).[20] Finds from the partially
excavated grave are still in the process of analysis, but once again there is evidence for
wide-ranging contacts, most notably a fine bone comb decorated with flowers which
Potts identifies as Bactrian (Potts 1993c). This find, together with the flask from Hili
Tomb A mentioned above, the Murghab seal recently published from Hamad Town in
Bahrain (Fig. 7.5), and other pieces such as the stone vessels from the foundation
deposit at the Barbar temple and the fine bull's head, all support the proposition that
relations of some sort existed between Arabia and Central Asia at this time (Crawford
and al Sindi 1995).

Other types of tombs can also be dated to the Umm-an-Nar period. Potts and Benton
have recently reported cremation burials from the outskirts of Dubai, at Tell es Sufouh,
associated with a standard Umm-an-Nar grave (Benton 1996). Two pits just outside the
perimeter of the tomb contained large numbers of cremated remains and it could be

[20] At Asimah Alignment A consisted of tombs and associated platforms on which ceremonies could also have taken place
(Vogt 1994).

7.5 A Murghab (Central Asian) seal in the National Museum Bahrain.

suggested that these were the bones of bodies originally deposited in the tomb itself which were then cleared to make room for more recently deceased members of the group. At Asimah unique alignments of subterranean graves have been excavated (Vogt 1994). At Ajman a 'classic' circular free-standing tomb was associated with a badly deflated settlement site and a second rectangular, subterranean, multiple burial of the same date. A rectangular tomb, Tomb N, is also reported from Hili associated with Tomb A. These rectangular graves are of particular interest as they foreshadow similar graves in the succeeding Wadi Suq period and indicate a degree of continuity between the two periods (al Tikriti 1989b: 95–7).

A rectangular grave dating to the Wadi Suq period, was excavated at Bidya 1, close to the Indian Ocean. It was a fine stone-built subterranean rectangular grave, twenty-five metres long, with multiple burials although the bones were so fragmentary that it is impossible to estimate the numbers. It had one highly unusual feature in that a lower chamber was found below the burial chamber. A number of remarkable objects were found in this grave. Six copper vessels had been deposited in the lower chamber, apparently as part of the funerary offerings, and a fine pectoral or pendant of gold showing two goats (Fig. 7.6) back to back came from the upper level (al Tikriti 1989b). Similar pieces are known from Qattarah, Shimal and Dhayah (see *AUAE* II–III: 44 for colour photographs). Reference has already been made to a copper goat pendant from Hamala North on Bahrain (chapter 5), while a little copper seahorse appliqué, apparently in a similar tradition, came from the earlier Umm-an-Nar settlement (Frifelt 1995: 196). Objects of precious metal are rare, although silver and gold beads occur from time to time. For instance, a collection of silver beads similar to examples from Hili, was found in the late Umm-an-Nar Tomb B at Ajman (al Tikriti 1989b).

A variety of burial rites are also found in the Wadi Suq period, the majority of which are multiple, although single and double inhumations in stone graves are known, again suggesting the possibility of a population of diverse cultural origins (for a summary see Potts 1990a: 237). The most impressive funerary monuments are the above ground stone tombs found at sites like Shimal, the largest of which has a length of twenty-seven

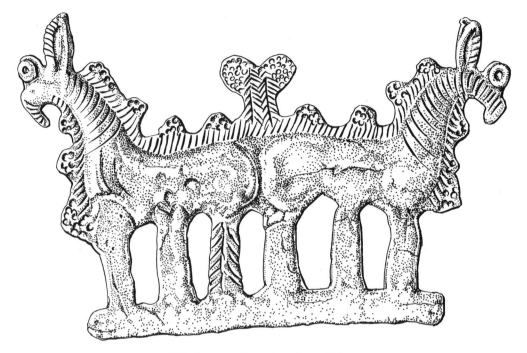

7.6 An animal pendant from Bidya.

metres. Their internal arrangements vary somewhat, some are single, some are double, most are rectangular, and the Shimal examples have rounded apsidal ends, some are divided longitudinally inside, and some seem to have been covered with a mound of gravel. They are built of vertical slabs of stone which form double walls filled with smaller stones, laid horizontally, a technique also seen in the last building at Hili III (see chapter 6). The inner wall inclines inwards so that more slabs can be laid across them to form a roof (Fig. 7.7). Many have a door in the centre of one of the long walls. The Shimal type of grave seems only to occur in a limited area which runs as far south as al Khatt. Other types have a wider distribution and seem to cover most of the UAE and Oman.

The range of grave goods in the Wadi Suq burials is similar to that from the Umm-an-Nar tombs, comprising pottery and stone vessels with a limited amount of metal-work and jewellery. Although the range is similar, the pottery in particular shows stylistic changes, as one would expect. It is significant that the range of foreign contacts indicated by these goods is rather different from that found in the earlier period. The contacts with Mesopotamia demonstrated at Umm-an-Nar island in particular, seem to have been replaced by contacts with the Indus valley, presumably reflecting the change in trading patterns known from the Mesopotamian texts at the end of the Ur III period, *c.* 2000 BC. This is the time when mention of Magan ceases in the

7.7 A grave of the Wadi Suq period at Shimal.

cuneiform record and the copper trade was channelled through Dilmun instead. It is possible that Magan attempted to compensate for this economic blow by developing its trade with the Indian subcontinent, so explaining the apparent increase in contacts. At Shimal, for instance, an Indus valley weight was found in Tomb 6, which also contained a Harappan jar (de Cardi 1988). Other contacts with the Indus are demonstrated by finds from the settlements such as Ras al Junayz on the Indian Ocean and will be discussed below. Not all the contacts were southwards, a certain amount of Barbar pottery of the Early Dilmun period has now been recovered from coastal sites in the UAE, most recently from Tell Abraq where this pottery is made from the same clay source as some of the pots from the site of Saar. The presence of this pottery must be connected with the transfer of copper from inland Oman to the new market place in Bahrain. No Mesopotamian pottery or other artefacts have been found, confirming the break in direct communications observed from the textual evidence.

It is curious that, in spite of losing the direct access to Mesopotamian markets, the change in overseas relations apparently had little effect on the economy or material prosperity of the peninsula. There is no evidence at all for an economic collapse. The continuing predominance of multiple burials, the continuity in the use of certain settlements and the absence of public buildings noted in the last chapter, all suggest that there is essential continuity between the two periods and that the organization of society changed little. It is also noticeable, however, that there is an apparent shift in settlement from the western slopes of the mountains to the eastern slopes and to the Indian Ocean coast. Further survey and excavation are necessary before this can be confirmed.

THE POTTERY

Inland and coastal sites of the Umm-an-Nar period are linked by the pottery and stone vessels found on them and by a limited range of copper artefacts. The first evidence for local pottery production dates to the early third millennium and it has been suggested that a high level of craft specialization can be identified. Craft specialization of this kind frequently indicates incipient stratification within society, something which is also indicated by the architecture. All the pottery is wheelmade and there is little technical development within the Hafit and Umm-an-Nar periods, apart from the introduction of a two-chambered kiln. The technical expertise of the Umm-an-Nar potters is demonstrated by the high quality of the pots they produced and by their skill in copying both fabric and decoration of wares from other areas like Iran (Méry 1991). The pottery of the Umm-an-Nar period can be divided into four broad groups; the domestic wares which are made of a sandy paste, often with a brownish/red slip, occasionally with applied decoration in the form of snakes or ribbons; the black on red fine painted wares; the black on grey painted wares and the foreign wares which can be found in each of the other groups. The range of shapes is limited in all groups and consists of simple bowls and globular jars, including a so-called canister. It is difficult to assess the true relative frequency of these groups as much of the evidence comes from graves, where the finer wares predominate and complete vessels are more likely to survive, thus skewing the picture.

The only stratified sequence covering the third millennium comes from the excavations at the tower house, Hili 8 and shows that the black on red wares date back to the Hafit period of the early third millennium, Hili period I, although all pottery remains scarce until the middle of Hili II, the Umm-an-Nar phase. At this period the sandy tempered domestic ware with simple linear painted decoration below the neck begins to appear in some quantity. Jars with applied ridges on the shoulder, sometimes pierced for suspension and even painted, are also present. Fine wares are very rare and show strong eastern affiliations. Even in the last phases of period II they only occur in tiny amounts; five incised grey ware sherds, a dozen black on grey ones and about sixty black on red sherds were retrieved, representing less than 1 per cent of the total corpus (Cleuziou 1989: 77).

A better idea of the quality and range of the pottery of the period can be gained from the contents of the graves, notably the well preserved remains from the lower part of Hili North Tomb A. Here more than 380 complete vessels were found and all four groups listed above are represented. The black on red ware with simple painted decoration on the top half of the vessel is again more plentiful than the black on grey ware, by contrast, occasional naturalistic motifs such as friezes of running caprids are found (see Fig. 3.3). Suspension jars in different fabrics represent 9 per cent of the complete vessels and are sometimes painted with a net pattern on the lower half of the pottery (Cleuziou and Vogt 1985).

Some comparable black on red sherds, apparently of Omani origin, have been found in south-east Iran, at Bampur and Tepe Yahya in contexts which date to the middle of the third millennium, and even further afield in eastern Iran at Shahr-i-Sokhta. In addition, some of the black on grey wares from Umm-an-Nar levels also show strong Iranian affinities, as does the incised grey ware, whose decoration seems to ape that of the earlier softstone vessels decorated in the so-called Intercultural style. Both the incised grey ware and some of the painted black on grey wares may even have originated in Iran, though Méry (1991) has demonstrated that the local potters were extremely skilled at 'faking' foreign wares. The presence of these copies seems to indicate that the supply of genuine foreign wares was inadequate to meet the demand and, perhaps, that supplies were unreliable.

The same range of shapes and decoration identified at Hili can also be seen on Umm-an-Nar island, but there is a marked contrast in the foreign wares identified here. At Umm-an-Nar island pots of undoubted southern Mesopotamian origin, almost unknown at Hili, are found in some quantity (Mynors 1983) and chain-ridge ware from Bahrain was also found from the settlement at the same site (Frifelt 1995: 186 Fig. 158). Conversely, black on red jars similar to those from Hili are known from a number of grave mounds on Bahrain and various types of Umm-an-Nar pottery come from City I levels on the Qalaʿat al Bahrain (Højlund and Andersen 1994). There must have been regular contacts between the three areas and this is, of course, the time when the Mesopotamian texts indicate close commercial relations with Magan. It is somewhat unexpected that none of these Mesopotamian pots seem to have penetrated inland where the copper, which was the basis of the trade, originated.

The coastal sites are also richer in sherds which are identified as Harappan in origin, many of which come from large storage jars with an everted rim and short neck. Indus valley pottery is found at the coastal site of Ras Ghanada in Abu Dhabi (al Tikriti 1985) and further south on the Indian Ocean at Ras al Hadd and Ras al Junayz, both sites which seem to date to the end of the Umm-an-Nar period, when, as we saw above, ties with the Indus valley became closer. Perhaps a little earlier in date, an etched carnelian bead was found in a grave at Umm-an-Nar. Other Indus valley traits are known from inland sites; two jars of fine black on red ware from Hili North Tomb A are decorated with the pipal leaf and the peacock, both typically Harappan motifs. Two etched carnelian beads were found in the same tomb (Cleuziou and Tosi 1989). These Harrapan artefacts do not occur in levels which predate the last quarter of the third millennium and seem to become more frequent in early second-millennium contexts, when, as discussed above, there was a change in the trade patterns.

Let us now return to the latest levels at Hili 8, known as period III, where there are important changes in both the architecture and the pottery corpus indicating that we are now in the succeeding Wadi Suq period, as it is called. The technical quality of the pottery deteriorates, though fine wares are still found, and is less well fired. The fabrics are varied and generally rather porous. They range in colour from buff to red. The pots are often slipped and string-cut bases become standard, having been rare in the earlier assemblage. The range of shapes and decoration remains limited. Perhaps the most common shapes are globular jars, often with wide trough spouts, bowls, and various simple beakers, some with round bases, some with low feet. The sequence at Abraq indicates that stemmed goblets become more common in the later part of the period (Potts 1990a). Decoration usually consists of lines or spirals confined to the top third of the vessel, though one charming beaker from grave 6 at Shimal is decorated with a frieze of running birds (de Cardi 1988) and other examples of naturalistic decoration are known.

The excavations at Abraq have also provided a number of pieces of imported Barbar ware, some of the earliest evidence for contacts between Dilmun and the Gulf of Oman. Both ridged ware and the fine red funerary ware has been found (Potts 1990a). Other similar sherds have been found at Ras Abaruk (de Cardi 1978) and in the Batinah. Contacts with the Indus valley continue and intensify. A Harrapan bottle jar with simple painted hoops round the shoulder was found in tomb 6 at Shimal with the weight which has already been mentioned, and some fingernail impressed sherds from Hili from both the end of period II and period III, are also thought to be Harrapan in origin (Cleuziou and Tosi 1989 Fig. 11). Wadi Suq wares have also been found in Bahrain and a sherd from Saar has a frieze of figures comparable to that on the Shimal beaker (Killick *et al.* 1991). Méry's findings on the skill of the Omani potters in reproducing foreign wares must not be forgotten when dealing with these purely stylistic criteria (Méry 1991). The parallels drawn should, where possible, be checked by analysis of the fabrics.

STONE VESSELS

As well as pottery, a wide range of stone vessels has been found in the area of Magan and as has been mentioned above, at least one manufacturing centre has been identified at Maysar, probably dating to the late third and early second millennia (Weisgerber 1981). Chlorite/steatite is found at a number of locations, often closely associated with deposits of copper, and other sorts of decorative stones are also available. It will be remembered that in the middle of the third millennium a very dis-

7.8 Steatite bowl of the Wadi Suq period.

tinctive type of decoration, called the Intercultural style, was found on softstone vessels which were found from Mari in the north, to Tepe Yahya in the east, and south as far as Tarut in the Eastern Province. At least one complete example is known from Bahrain, but very few pieces have been identified from Oman or the UAE. Two pieces come from Umm-an-Nar island (see p. 127). The majority of the third-millennium vessels from the Oman peninsula are simple shapes decorated with incised lines and the dot and circle motif. In addition to hemispherical bowls, some with spouts, and 'canisters' we find rectangular, compartmented boxes of a type also found in Iran at the site of Shahdad. Lids are also common with a stalk-like handle and a recessed rim. These too are decorated with the ubiquitous dot and circle. This style has been called *série récente* by Miroschedji (1973) to distinguish it from the earlier figurative style.

More recently Vogt and Potts have adopted the description *série intermédiaire* to separate out the very similar softstone corpus from the early second millennium which is distinguished by the predominance of round-bodied suspension vessels with the vertically pierced lugs placed about two-thirds of the way down the body (Fig. 7.8). However, Häser has implied that the difference may be geographical rather than chronological as biconical vessels are concentrated in the UAE while globular ones are commonly found in Oman and northwards as far as Failaka (Häser 1990). One example was found in a house at Mohenjo-Daro (Cleuziou and Tosi 1989: 41, Fig. 12). Zigzag decoration is now found in addition to the dot and circle, and double circles with dots become more common. One or two more exotic pieces may point again to eastern Iran and Bactria where there was also a popular industry manufacturing softstone vessels (Potts 1993c).

METAL

The economic importance of copper mining has been mentioned a number of times, but it is well known that the dating of mining sites in the pre-industrial era is extremely difficult. Techniques of extraction changed little until modern times and dateable artefacts in the mines are scarce. The evidence in Oman and the UAE for the commercial exploitation of the plentiful deposits of copper probably goes back to the Hafit period in the late fourth millennium, a time when copper first seems to have been imported into Mesopotamia from the Gulf region (Hauptmann *et al*. 1988: 35). The evidence for this early exploitation is mainly indirect and comes from the graves which are found on ridges close to easily accessible deposits. At Maysar, for instance, the adits, or horizontal shafts, at Maysar 2 probably date back to the Hafit period to judge from the presence of tombs of this age on the surrounding ridges. Umm-an-Nar graves are also present at Maysar 4 so the workings probably continued in use. It is only in the later third millennium that we have direct evidence for their use with the building of the settlement at Maysar 1. In the houses are mauls and hammerstones used for breaking up the smelted copper and twenty-two bun-shaped ingots weighing more than six kilograms were found in House 4. It has been calculated that between 2,000–4,000 tons of copper were smelted in the third to second millennia (Hauptmann *et al*. 1988: 47). The evidence from Maysar suggests that the initial smelting was probably carried out close to the mines, where timber was available, and further work on refining the metal and making the ingots was done in the settlements. Similar evidence comes from the site of Zahra north-west of Sohar (Costa and Wilkinson 1987).

The early mining activity must have been somewhat experimental and slags dating to the earliest period of extraction in the Hafit still contain as much as 31 per cent copper. By the Umm-an-Nar period techniques had improved considerably and only about 2 per cent remains in the waste (Hauptmann *et al*. 1988: 37). Analysis of the ingots shows high levels of both arsenic and nickel in the copper which would have enhanced its casting properties. Similarly high levels of nickel were noted in many of the artefacts from the Royal Cemetery at Ur which is in part at least contemporary with the Umm-an-Nar period. The date of the earliest tin bronze in the Arabian peninsula is still unclear, but probably also dates to the Umm-an-Nar period. Copper alloyed with 5 per cent tin was recovered from the metal-working area close to the tower house at Hili 8 in level IIf at the end of the period (Cleuziou 1989: 74). There is little tin in Oman and the evidence discussed above for contacts with Central Asia suggests that it may have come from as far away as Afghanistan, possibly via the Indus.

Metal objects have not survived well from the early part of the Umm-an-Nar period and in spite of the evidence quoted above for mining activity there are surprisingly few artefacts. Artefacts from the third millennium generally consist of small items such as pins and finger rings, with occasional copper seals or pendants like a tiny example from Ras Ghanada (al Tikriti 1985: Pl 16a). Tools and blades are also found; Maysar 25 produced a fine chisel and a large flat blade came from grave 3 at Maysar 4 (Weisgerber 1981: 198 and 204). Beads, nails and a variety of blades are also known from sites in this area, while copper fishhooks occur on coastal sites. Spearheads have been found at a number of Umm-an-Nar sites, including the Asimah graves, and sometimes have a raised midrib on the head, which has a diamond-shaped cross-section. The shaft is hollow and made of sheet metal beaten round the haft and sometimes riveted on. This

7.9 A copper goblet from Asimah.

type of blade has a long life and occurs into the second millennium as well. Two examples were found driven vertically into the ground close to tomb 102 at Shimal and so probably date to the period around 2000 BC. Identical examples were found on Bahrain, probably a little later in date (Killick *et al.* 1991: 124). Arrowheads with a flattened midrib, sometimes incised with Xs, and a square-sectioned tang are also widely distributed by the second millennium and a collection of twenty-four of them came also from tomb 102 at Shimal (Vogt and Franke-Vogt 1987: 26 and 34). Arrowheads such as these also occur in the succeeding Iron Age so that there would seem to be a strong conservative tradition amongst the local metal-workers.

More exotic metal objects also occur from time to time such as the decorative plaques in gold, silver and copper described above. A few copper vessels are also known of which perhaps the earliest is a copper goblet from Alignment A at Asimah (Vogt 1994: 120, Fig. 55) which is identical to an example from Hamala north on Bahrain (Fig. 7.9). During-Caspers has suggested that this type of vessel is an import from the Indus (1991). Recent excavations at Bidya recovered six bronze containers, two of which had rounded bases and single handles riveted onto the body, which suggested to the excavator that they might have been used as dippers or scoops. A similar vessel has been found at Shimal. In addition, there were two simple bowls and two other vessels which seem to have been footed goblets (al Tikriti 1989a: 106). In the late Umm-an-Nar grave at Ajman B are other exotic goods like the two etched carnelian beads mentioned above (al Tikriti 1989c). The furnishings of this grave are unusual as two steatite (?) seals were also found. Both were of poor quality, one a stamp seal with a net pattern of incised lines, the second a cylinder seal with no discernible pattern.

SEALS

Seals are rare in Oman and the UAE and, of the few examples known, none can with certainty be said to be of local manufacture. A recently discovered example from Tell Abraq may represent local workmanship as no close parallels are known (Potts 1993d: 434). Others, such as a circular stamp seal from Maysar and another pear-shaped one, seem to have some affinity with Central Asian examples; a triangular example from the same site can be matched in the Indus Valley (Weisgerber 1980: 105, 1981: 218–9) and a classic Dilmun seal was found in a grave at Mazyad (Cleuziou 1981: 285). Three more, now lost, were found just north of the Rub al Khali near Nadqan (Golding 1974). Another bifacial seal or pendant was found in an uncertain context at Shimal and is compared by the excavator to one from Failaka (Vogt and Franke-Vogt 1987: 82). More recently, four seals have been reported from Ras al Junayz (Cleuziou *et al.* 1994). One of these is an unusual square copper seal of Harappan origin, while the other three are made of recycled softstone, apparently from locally-made vases and a lid. Of these, two have symbols on them which may be a form of proto-writing, while the third and largest has a scene showing two men and a branch or frond in a style rather similar to that found in the reliefs on the Umm-an-Nar graves of the later third millennium. The C14 dates from the site would agree with this dating.

Seals as we have seen above, occur seldom and to date no sealings have been recovered so we have no clues as to how they were used. Weights are known, but are imported examples from the Indus valley, underlining again the importance of contacts with this region in the late third and early second millennia. Examples have been found at Tell Abraq (Potts 1993a) and as already mentioned, at tomb 6 at Shimal. Except for the Harappan signs on the triangular seal from Maysar, on the copper seal from Ras al Junayz and those scratched on potsherds from the same site, there is little trace of a recording system either. We must not, however, forget the proto-writing on two other seals from Ras al Junayz. All these factors taken in conjunction suggest that bureaucracy does not seem to have played much of a role in the economy of the area. This in turn would support the model of a decentralized small-scale society with little formal organizational structure.

SUMMARY

The Umm-an-Nar and Wadi Suq periods together probably lasted more than 1500 years. There is a strong thread of continuity between them, but it is unsurprising that fundamental changes also occur over such a long time span. The third millennium saw a rapid increase in the numbers of permanent settlements as agricultural techniques improved. The growing demand for copper meant that many of these new settlements were within easy reach of the mines and some of them, like Maysar, continued in use into the Wadi

Suq period. The settlements at Hili 8 and at Abraq also continue and what is probably a new settlement appears at Shimal, although it is possible that an earlier village existed here, too, as a few sherds of Umm-an-Nar pottery have been identified. The distribution of sites also seems to alter, with more evidence for occupation on the Indian Ocean coast from the late Umm-an-Nar period, but it must be remembered that survey is very patchy and that the processes of wind erosion and redeposition make it very likely that other sites of both periods remain to be found, while some have been totally destroyed. The present state of the evidence indicates that the number of permanent settlements dwindled in the course of the second millennium and it appears that only Abraq survives by the second half of the millennium. It has been suggested that the economic decline initiated by the collapse of the copper trade with Mesopotamia in the early second millennium led to a gradual abandonment of agricultural villages and a return to a nomadic way of life. It may be possible to identify the beginnings of this change during the later Umm-an-Nar period.

Other continuities also exist between Umm-an-Nar and Wadi Suq, most importantly in the burials. The presence of subterranean, rectangular graves contemporary with the more numerous 'classic' Umm-an-Nar graves has already been mentioned, as together they foreshadow the developments in the Wadi Suq period when multiple burials in rectangular free-standing graves are an important feature. (Single and double graves are also found and the distinction between them may be a geographical one.) The identification of a number of different burial rites in use simultaneously suggests a diverse population, each section of which had its own customs. Other links between the two periods can be seen in the softstone repertoire which shows a gradual development over time, with no evidence for abrupt change. The same is true of the pottery where, for example, spiral decoration and string-cut bases, both typical of the Wadi Suq pots, have now been identified at Hili in the Umm-an-Nar period (Cleuziou 1989).

The material culture of the whole area shows a certain uniformity by the middle of the third millennium, but there is no evidence for political integration. The Umm-an-Nar period has provided some pointers to the organization of society, and nothing from the Wadi Suq period contradicts these. There is no evidence for urban settlement in either period. Frifelt and Orchard have both suggested that urban sites were present, (Frifelt 1976; Orchard and Stranger 1994) but although the buildings are scattered over as much as 300 hectares in some areas there is no evidence for density of settlement, or for the presence of specialized activity areas and public buildings within these enclaves, all of which are essential if a site is to meet the generally recognized criteria for defining urban status (Childe 1950). There are no palaces, temples, or administrative centres. There is no convincing evidence for a stratified society or for full time specialists, except perhaps for potters. The evidence of the graves in which even base metals are somewhat unusual points to a fairly egalitarian distribution of wealth, consonant with a familial or clan-based social structure. There is very little evidence of formal administrative systems and even less for a native recording system. In these circumstances it is difficult to see how such a large and fragmented geographical area could be considered as a political entity.

Available evidence suggests a very different kind of society from that on Bahrain, one composed, perhaps, of semi-autonomous local groups of tribal or extended family units under the rule of a chief or *shaikh*. The settlement pattern in the Umm-an-Nar period is one of scattered villages in oases or close to important natural resources like copper. These villages are often dominated by one or more tower houses round which unfortified dwellings are found. It has been suggested that some of the tower houses may have housed the head of the community, or the heads of the main families in areas where more than one main family occurs. It was also suggested that some of those towers without internal structures may have been corrals to protect the stock of the village from attack. The traces of flimsy houses of perishable materials, in addition to the more permanent structures, suggests that additional temporary occupation may also have occurred at certain times of the year. There are no indisputable public buildings and no evidence for a formal religious system, though the care taken over the burial of the dead strongly suggests a belief in the afterlife.

In some cases multiple burials are closely associated with the tower houses, as at Hili and Abraq, and probably housed members of the same extended family. It is this unit which was the basic building block of the society. The grave goods are not particularly rich, gold and silver are rare in both the Umm-an-Nar and Wadi Suq periods. A striking exception is the gold pendant from Qattarah (Fig. 7.10). The dead do, however, seem to have been provided with a respectable quantity of pots and softstone vessels, as well as other personal belongings like rings and weapons. The picture generally is of a comfortable but not luxurious existence. The tombs do not by themselves indicate the presence of full time specialists, although their size and elaboration must mean a degree of expertise and of cooperation within the local community.

The material culture presents the same sort of picture, although Méry (1991) has argued for the presence of professional potters. The copper-working is apparently simple, remains of the smelting process is found in almost all the houses excavated at Maysar 1 and the variable quality of the copper ingots is frequently referred to in the cuneiform documents, suggesting a lack of 'quality control' and a fairly low level of technical competence (Moorey 1994). There is no evidence for the use of complex metal-working processes such as *cire perdue* casting. This simple technology also indicates a non-specialized, non-stratified society, organized perhaps on a familial basis.

These semi-autonomous villages were not isolated. The uniformity seen in the pottery, metalwork and softstone vessels shows quite clearly that there were close contacts between them, but it is suggested that these contacts were commercial rather than political and that they may have been facilitated by the nomadic or semi-nomadic elements in society. The nature of the region with a range of specialized ecological niches

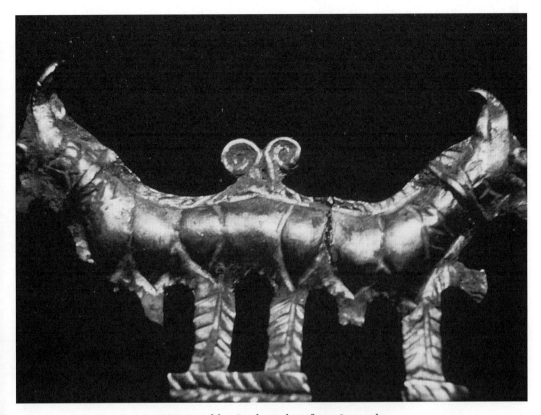

7.10 A gold animal pendant from Qattarah.

producing valuable raw materials and different types of foodstuffs, coupled with a harsh climate where local fluctuations in temperature and precipitation can be economically disastrous, makes local trade a necessity. Exchange of local goods and redistribution of foreign ones, facilitated by family connections, together with a limited number of production centres for pottery and softstone, would explain the cultural integration observed in the two periods.

The importance of foreign trade is a constant feature throughout the two periods under consideration although the pattern changes. As we have seen, the early contacts in the Hafit period were with Mesopotamia and reached the inland mining centres. By the middle of the third millennium contact with Mesopotamia seems to be confined to coastal sites like Umm-an-Nar, suggesting that the copper was being exchanged here rather than at the mines. Slightly later Harappan goods begin to appear both inland and on the coast, though it is not clear what the Harappans received in exchange. The finds of blocks of bitumen at Ras al Junayz suggest other goods which may have been traded (Cleuziou *et al.* 1994). This connection with the Indus valley superseded that with Mesopotamia in importance *c.* 2000 BC and its commercial influence is seen in the use of Indus valley weights in Magan and in the presence of the Indus seal at Ras al Junayz. The importance of the trade with the Indus continues to increase in the period after the fall of the Ur III dynasty in Mesopotamia about 2000 BC when the cuneiform records indicate that direct contacts with Oman/Magan cease. It declines with the decline of the Harappan civilization.

By the Isin-Larsa period, *c.* 2000–1800 BC, Mesopotamia was dealing solely with Dilmun to acquire its copper. It is generally assumed that Dilmun, which had no copper of its own, was importing it from Magan. It is therefore surprising that relatively little Early Dilmun pottery has yet been found on the coast of the Emirates, though work at Abraq and on the Batinah shows that such contacts existed. Apart from the Dilmun seals at Mazyad and Nadqan, there is very little evidence for contact between Dilmun and inland Magan either. The loss of direct contacts with Mesopotamia may have been one of the reasons for the apparent decline in prosperity in Oman which is shown by the decline of permanent settlement in the region during the Wadi Suq period. On the other hand, it is possible we are seeing a shift in the population eastwards rather than a decline in the total number of settlements.

The dating of the end of the Wadi Suq period is still a matter for discussion, but it seems increasingly likely that it lasted until the third quarter of the second millennium and merged imperceptibly with the succeeding Iron Age. The stylistic links which can be demonstrated in the metalwork and in the softstone vases make it unlikely that there was a complete hiatus between the two periods.

Chapter 8

DILMUN, DEVELOPMENT AND DECLINE.
AN OVERVIEW

In spite of the upsurge in archaeological activity in the Gulf region summarized in pre-vious chapters, it will be obvious that the evidence relating to the most important years of the Early Dilmun period is still very fragmentary. There are many questions that we cannot begin to answer. We have next to no evidence on settlement pattern for instance, nor is there a realistic hope of obtaining it, due to the physical conditions in the area, and to the extremely rapid rate of development. On Bahrain, for example, survey has located a proportion of the sites and the approximate position of others can be tentatively deduced from the positions of the surviving mound fields, but the sizes of the sites, their functions and their relationship to each other are lost. The loss of this information makes any attempt at central place analysis impossible and deprives us of one crucial tool in the attempt to recreate and understand the way man was using his environment.

The emphasis of archaeological research in Dilmun itself has often been on the rescue excavation of mounds or other burials and even where settlements have been studied excavation has been confined to small areas. Until the LBAE's excavations at Saar began, no horizontal exposure of a site of the period had been extensive enough to allow analy-sis of the use of space within a settlement. No critical analysis of domestic housing had been attempted either, because of the lack of information. The only public buildings uncovered to date in the Early Dilmun period are temples, although it is possible that the earliest phase of the palace at Failaka dates back to this period. The wall around City II is further evidence for public works. There is no evidence for administrative build-ings and very little for manufacturing areas. We are still fumbling in the dark. This has led to the evidence from Saar being treated in this book as representative of all settle-ment in Dilmun, simply because there is nothing else, but the possibility that this small town with its amazingly orderly layout is some kind of special function site must not be forgotten. A case could be made for its being a planned settlement on the lines of the more or less contemporary workmen's village at Lahun in Egypt. The evidence from the Oman peninsula suffers from the same limitations, so that the present attempt to summarize and contrast the development of the two regions must be seen as a first attempt at building models which will require rigorous testing in the future as more facts become available. Areas for future study will also be highlighted.[22]

---

[22] Detailed references for the conclusions presented in the first part of this summary will be found in relevant sections of the earlier chapters.

ENVIRONMENT AND ECONOMY

Evidence for the physical conditions in the upper Gulf and for the subsistence strategies used by people of Dilmun is now slowly being collected. Studies of the coastline indicate that the sea level was initially as much as ten metres higher than at present, but began falling during the period covered by this book. This changing sea level would have had consequences for fresh water supplies as well as for the positioning of harbours and waterways. Much of the data is still in the process of analysis and it is clear that the picture changes considerably from one part of the Gulf to another. There is no evidence for significant climatic change.

The outlines of the subsistence base are now clear, and its flexibility throughout the region is striking. Hunting, fishing, and garden agriculture are found and in the Oman peninsula these are augmented by copper extraction. All these strategies are complementary thus providing a flexible response to a harsh environment. The nature and extent of irrigation is still unclear, although the crops grown and the ditches associated with many of the tower houses in Oman are good indications of its presence. Orchard has suggested that some type of *qanāt* system may already have been employed in the Oman peninsula, but no physical remains of such a system have yet been identified (Orchard and Stranger 1994: 87). On Bahrain however, the new work at Umm-es-Sejour suggests that something more than simple above ground channels running from wells to the fields may have been known (Konishi 1994: 19, Fig. 5). The answer to this question will help to assess, amongst other things, how much grain could have been grown locally and how much was being imported. Potts in a recent article has shown convincingly that there is no evidence for a large scale trade in barley (Potts 1993d). In addition, dental evidence suggests that cereals may not have played a major role in the diet. The many *tannurs*, querns and grinders found at Early Dilmun sites would suggest some level of general consumption, although all can be used for processing materials other than cereals. Garden produce, especially dates, was extremely important and date stones provide by far the most plentiful palaeobotanical evidence, together with remains of the leaves and wood of the palm. Other seed remains are scarce, apparently because of local soil conditions which have led to poor preservation, but fruits such as melon are present.

Bone, on the other hand, survives well, and domestic animals are generally well documented. It has been suggested, because of the range of size observed in the remains from Saar which suggests a varied population, that there was a trade in sheep which were imported into Bahrain (Dobney and Jaques 1994). Cattle were present in small numbers and were probably used for traction. Pig and dog bones are rare and this raises the question of how the cervids, whose bones are also found in small numbers, were hunted. Without dogs they may have been trapped. At the Qalaʿat it seems that the dogs themselves were eaten (Uerpmann and Uerpmann in Højlund and Andersen

1994). Evidence for the presence of the camel has also been found and Hoch thinks it is probable that it was domesticated by the middle of the third millennium (Hoch in Frifelt 1995: 252).

The importance of marine resources has been repeatedly stressed and it should not be forgotten that fish was traditionally used in the Gulf region as fodder for animals and as fertilizer, in addition to providing food for man himself. The variety of species found indicates that a number of different fishing techniques were used and in addition to hooks, for which there is direct archaeological evidence, nets and traps were almost certainly known. Ethnographic evidence points to a long tradition of fixed trap nets. Both inshore and deep water fish are found so more than one method of fishing may have been employed. In addition, molluscs and sea mammals contributed valuable raw materials in addition to protein, and pearls, tortoiseshell and dugong ivory are all found.

Other easily accessible natural resources in the region included above all copper, stone of variable quality and flint. The copper and the softstone used for both seals and bowls came from a number of sources on the Arabian peninsula outside Dilmun, as did some of the semi-precious stones used for beads. Agate and carnelian are both said to occur. Small amounts of bitumen are found on the mainland of Kuwait and on both Failaka and Bahrain; clay and salt are widely available, as is poor quality wood from the omnipresent palm trees which also provided fibres for rope and leaves from which mats and baskets were made. Mangrove was also used, while high quality timber had to be imported. Pearls were probably exploited from Ubaid times. The region as a whole was well provided with raw materials, although their localized distribution again encouraged the economic interdependence which has already been noted.

SOCIAL STRUCTURE

It is suggested that the societies which developed in the Gulf in the middle of the third millennium based on this mixed economy which utilized farming, fishing and hunting, and which traded for the goods they lacked, were diverse and that contrasts can be drawn between the northern Gulf area, based on Dilmun, and the Oman peninsula. In Dilmun we can suggest the presence of a relatively unstratified society, probably of diverse origins, based in the main on the nuclear family as the basic unit. Support for this model comes both from the graves and from domestic architecture. The mounds, which are the normal burial rite for the Dilmun period, seldom hold more than ten individuals, and usually hold fewer, again probably representing a family group. Unfortunately the human remains are rarely well enough preserved to determine the ages and sexes of the dead. The grave complexes, of which two were found near Saar, suggest that some sections of society were organized in larger extended family or tribal groupings. Where the contents of the graves survive they are not luxurious, usually consisting of personal belongings and offerings of food and drink. The only graves which vary from this rule are the so-called Royal graves at A'ali.

Evidence from both Failaka and Saar shows that, by the early second millennium, the basic domestic unit was a small, rectangular building in a terrace of similar ones, each only big enough for a nuclear family. Expansion of the family by births or marriages seems to have been catered for by breaking through into the neighbouring house and absorbing an additional unit. The furnishings of these houses and their dimensions are fairly standardized and do not suggest major differences in wealth. Nor is there evidence from the houses or from the artefacts found for a high degree of craft specialization. However, the standardized nature of the pottery strongly suggests that this was mass produced by professionals. The absence of locally produced, luxury wares, even in the graves, also argues against a strongly differentiated society. There seems to have been little demand for such a ware and the limited need was met by imported pottery, much of it, like the goblets from A'ali for example, with Indo-Iranian links, while other painted wares seem to have originated in Oman.

The evidence provided by the other main crafts gives a mixed picture. Simple copper-working certainly took place in most of the excavated settlements, but the copper seems to have been imported as ingots and the articles made were mainly simple pins, hooks and chisels made by casting in an open mould and hammering. A high degree of technical skill was not necessary to produce such items. A copper-working area was identified within one of the domestic units at Saar by the 1988 Bahraini/Jordanian expedition. A kiln and fragments of ingots were found in the L-shaped outer section of one of the houses (al Sindi pers. comm.). This seems to point towards a cottage industry in this instance. We cannot be sure on the limited evidence what the status of metalworkers was.

On the other hand, a case can be made for the presence of skilled masons employed to build both graves and public buildings, though they may not have been full time specialists. The quality of the stonework on the second Barbar temple and on some of the drum-shaped graves certainly indicates a considerable level of skill. The seals, too, must have been produced by specialists, possibly from a single workshop in each area, in order to avoid repetition of designs. One such workshop was identified in City II at the Qala'at and another on Failaka.

There is one other class of specialist for whom there is convincing evidence and that is the priest. The number and variety of temples is remarkable, considering the limited amount of excavation which has taken place, and their physical prominence shows that they were clearly of importance to the settlements they served. There seems to have been no canonical form for the buildings or for their fixtures and fittings. It has been suggested that water may have played an important role in the religion, but it is only at Barbar that a well is firmly enclosed within a temple compound. At Umm-es-Sejour the 'shrine' may be no more than an altar and some guardian figures set up at this important spring. No other buildings have yet been identified associated with wells or springs. Neither at Saar, nor at Diraz, does water seem to have played an important role. At F3 on Failaka two water storage tanks were discovered in the square building which has been tentatively identified as a temple, but these may have been practical rather than ideological.

All except the Failaka 'temple' have altars where offerings were made to the deity. Traces of burnt fish and dates associated with the altars suggest the offering of food and drink, while the presence of two altars at Saar raises the possibility that a divine couple were worshipped here. The only divine couple known from the texts are Inzak and his wife Meskilak, but our information is so limited that we cannot be certain that they were the couple to whom the Saar temple was dedicated. The range of temple plans in Dilmun, and the variety of the fittings, points to a pantheon of gods and we can guess that they represented natural forces, a guess supported by the iconography of the seals where sun disks and crescents are commonly found associated with divine figures or their standards.

The grounds for associating the Sumerian water god Ea/Enki with Dilmun rest largely on the Mesopotamian textual evidence and on a seal from Bahrain apparently showing a god in an underground chamber, thought by some to be Ea in his Apsu. It could equally represent a local water god. No doubt Dilmun had a rich repertoire of local myths and stories woven round its own gods and glimpses of such stories can be found on the seals. One seal from Saar (5168:01), shows a dramatic scene of the stabbing of a seated god by a human figure while another looks on in horror. Only if we retrieve local texts can we hope to understand these scenes. Attempts to interpret the religion of Dilmun in terms of that of Mesopotamia should be viewed with great caution.

Reference has repeatedly been made to the apparently organized nature of society in the Early Dilmun period, but no evidence has yet been put forward as to the method of organization. There is indeed very little which can be produced. The presence of an apparently fully urban centre at the Qalaʿat and of a network of other settlements, including the ones on Failaka, with an identical material culture, argues for the existence of some formal structure to integrate this complex system. For example, the motifs on the seals from Failaka, apparently made on the island itself, are drawn from the same repertoire as those from Bahrain and yet do not repeat them. The long-distance trade for which Dilmun was well known also suggests some central authority as such systems require standardization of weights, values and practices.

The presence at Aʿali of a group of burial mounds much larger and apparently originally much more richly furnished than any others we know of, supports the presence of such an authority, but does not help us to elucidate its nature. There are few clues in Dilmun itself as to what this authority might have been. The lack of fortified tower houses such as those we saw in Oman and the predominance of nuclear family graves and houses may argue against government by tribal shaiks. With one possible exception, the only non-domestic buildings identified in the Dilmun period are religious, which might suggest that the priests were the force behind the organization of society. As yet however, little evidence for administrative activity has been found associated with the temples. It could be suggested that the merchants or the heads of the major families formed some sort of oligarchy, but the presence of the Aʿali graves argues against this. One might expect such people to be buried in the richest grave in the cemetery nearest to their home, not all together in one place.

The only direct evidence there is for the nature of the central authority comes from the cuneiform sources. A text from Mari dating to the Old Assyrian empire refers to the issue of two litres of cypress essence for a king, 'lugal', of Dilmun (Groneberg 1992). If this one text is to be taken at face value then Dilmun was a monarchy and the graves at Aʿali can be seen as truly royal. Some uncertainties still remain: what exactly did the Mari scribes understand by the word 'lugal'; why have no palace-type buildings been found on Bahrain, in the Eastern Province or in the early levels at Failaka; why are there are no identifiable representations of kingly figures on seals[23] or on the very limited amount of other forms of representational art known? It would be rash to assume that this problem has been solved on the basis of a single text.

Another set of questions needs to be raised about the relationship between Bahrain and the so-called colony on Failaka. By about 1900 BC the evidence for Dilmun being, as Højlund has suggested (1994: 474), a single political entity encompassing the three geographical areas of Failaka, Bahrain and the Eastern Province is compelling. The uniformity of the material culture, and especially of the administrative tools, over such a wide geographical area is difficult to explain in any other way. This uniformity also points strongly in the direction of a centralized administration, but we do not know if Failaka was under direct rule from the Qalaʿat or whether it may have had semi-independent status.

THE OMAN PENINSULA

The evidence presented in chapters 6 and 7 presents a very different picture from that which has just been painted of Dilmun in the late third and early second millennia. Once again, in Oman and the UAE, a large geographical area is linked by a similar, though not identical material culture. The absence of urban centres and of identifiable administrative tools suggests that the observed similarities are probably the result of local economic exchange networks rather than of central control. The settlement pattern here seems to have been non-urban and widely scattered throughout the Early Dilmun period. Dispersed groups of buildings, usually dominated by one or more

---

[23] One or two presentation scenes showing a person standing before a 'king' are known from Failaka, but they seem to belong to a slightly later period. See, for example, Pic in Calvet and Gaschet 1990: 137: 18.

tower houses, are typical of the oases until the beginning of the second millennium, when many of them are deserted. Other flimsier buildings have also been identified, perhaps the remains of temporary housing, but no incontrovertible evidence has yet been found for administrative or other public buildings. The presence of massive, stone-built graves containing up to 200 burials, sometimes closely associated with the tower houses, may indicate a tribal or extended family system not unlike that of today. The evidence for settlement in the early second millennium is very sparse, although multiple burials continue, showing some continuity with what had gone before.

As in Dilmun, evidence for craft specialization or a stratified society is slight. Potters and stonemasons may have been full time professionals, miners and metalworkers also, though the techniques they employed are fairly crude and seasonal working by transhumant groups is another possibility; itinerant craftsmen may also have been present. The evidence from Maysar for the Wadi Suq period shows an area of the village devoted to stone bowl manufacture, but we cannot tell if it was permanently inhabited. We do not even have evidence for priests, although the care taken in the disposal of at least some of the dead may suggest their presence. Seals are very rare and there are no other administrative or recording devices of local origin, perhaps because there was no need for them, or because they were of perishable materials. The negative evidence, together with such slight evidence as we have for settlement and burial, supports the case for saying that society here was a loosely knit web of tribal or extended family groups, led by chiefs or shaikhs. These groups were economically interdependent but lacking in formal governmental structures.

DILMUN AND MAGAN AS A TRADING PARTNERS

It has been repeatedly said that Dilmun owed its prosperity, and probably its existence as a political entity, to its geographical position athwart a major line of communication between Mesopotamia and the Indian sub-continent. This position was made especially valuable by the presence within its borders of sheltered harbours and fresh water, both essentials for successful maritime voyages before the advent of steam. The island of Bahrain was especially well-endowed in this respect. Magan, on the other hand, was primarily an end supplier of raw materials and also, to a limited extent, of manufactured goods. It may at times have served as a staging post for goods from the Indus valley.

The pattern of contacts between Dilmun, Magan and their trading partners is not stable and over the 3,000 years or so covered by this book a number of important changes can be documented. The earliest contacts, dating to the middle part of the Ubaid period (the middle to late fifth millennium), are between southern Mesopotamia and the eastern seaboard of Arabia, as far south as Abu Dhabi and Sharjah. One site has also been excavated on Bahrain. From these coastal areas some pieces of Ubaid pottery were diffused inland, but there is no evidence to suggest that people from Mesopotamia were involved in this latter process. Masry's spheres of interaction model fits the evidence for the dissemination of goods from the coast to inland sites well, but it is less easy to tell how Ubaid pottery was transmitted to the coastal sites in the first instance. Contacts seem to have been spasmodic and may have resulted from boats travelling in both directions. Such journeys would have been made by hopping from one coastal site to another. The prevailing north-westerly wind suggests that it would have been easier to travel south from Mesopotamia than northwards against the winds, so we can tentatively suggest that contacts may well have been initiated by sailors from the north.

The evidence from Dilmun for contacts in the succeeding Uruk period of Mesopotamia (fourth millennium) is sparse, and at present is confined to a limited amount of pottery from the Eastern Province of Arabia and one or two possible sherds from Bahrain; there are also a limited number of textual references from Uruk itself. There is no evidence at all from the Oman peninsula. Contacts appear to have remained spasmodic throughout most of the fourth millennium and it is suggested that this was because the main thrust of Mesopotamian trade in the Uruk period was north and north-west into Anatolia. By the end of the Uruk period this picture changes dramatically. The Euphrates route collapsed and at about the same time the first textual references to Dilmun, already coupled with copper, are found in southern Mesopotamia. Jemdat Nasr pottery of Mesopotamian origin, dating to the end of the fourth millennium and the beginning of the third, occurs in the Hafit graves of the Oman peninsula, the earliest built structures from this region.

This raises the problem of the exact location of Dilmun at this period: the texts refer to Dilmun, the archaeological evidence comes from Oman. We can suggest two possible explanations: the first that the name Dilmun referred to an area which included Oman at this early time and may have meant nothing more specific than 'Lands to the south', and the second that the copper was being acquired from the mines in Oman by people in the Eastern Province, an area later known to be part of Dilmun, who were then passing it on to Mesopotamia (Bahrain appears to have been virtually uninhabited at this period). Given the scarcity of archaeological evidence from the Eastern Province it is hard to believe that this was the case, and direct contact between Oman and southern Mesopotamia is a more likely explanation. Significantly, Jemdat Nasr pottery is distributed along the routes linking the coast to the rich, inland copper mining areas of Oman. A wider meaning for the term Dilmun at this time to include Oman, seems to follow from the archaeological evidence.

This direct contact between Mesopotamia and Oman appears to have continued into the first half of the third millennium as considerable quantities of Early Dynastic period pottery have been found on Umm-an-Nar island and at Abraq, both sites where copper collected from the mines of Oman was apparently exchanged. The main overseas contacts of the flourishing inland sites seem, by contrast, to have been with Iran and, after about 2500 BC, with the Indus valley. These contacts may have been made via the Indian Ocean coast. Early Dynastic wares have also been found in the Eastern Province and by the middle of the millennium the first arguably urban site in the peninsula is located here at Tarut. The texts continue to list Dilmun as a source of building timbers and copper.

We are faced with the same dilemma as with the fourth millennium evidence. Should Dilmun still be seen as a non-specific blanket term or not? It can be suggested that by the middle of the third millennium, with the emergence of Tarut as a manufacturing centre for chlorite bowls and a stopover on the route up or down the Gulf, this area was beginning to assert its economic muscle. The earliest permanent settlements also appear on Bahrain at the same time and the presence in them of a relatively high proportion of wares of Mesopotamian origin, as much as 19 per cent in period Ib at the Qala'at al Bahrain, point to its rising importance in the international trade network. On the other hand, the unequivocal evidence for Mesopotamian wares at Umm-an-Nar in the UAE, indicates that Dilmun was still a rather general term. It is perhaps significant that it is soon after this, in the Agade period, that the names Magan and Meluhha first appear. We can suggest that as the trade built up in volume and sailors from Mesopotamia became better acquainted with the Gulf, they began to distinguish between its component parts, in particular between Magan, the Oman peninsula, and Dilmun to the north. The name Dilmun was probably restricted to the Eastern Province and Bahrain by the third quarter of the third millennium. By the end of the millennium it also included Failaka.

If we accept this explanation one further problem still remains: the precise location of Magan. At least three of the Agade rulers campaigned against it. Naram-Sin claimed to have campaigned in Magan, to have captured its ruler (en), and to have taken back diorite for use in making royal statues. In addition, we have the inscription of Manishtusu in which he claims victory over the rulers of thirty-two towns 'on the other side of the sea' and says that he brought back silver and black stone as booty. This campaign is interpreted by some scholars as referring to Magan (Potts T. 1994: 104–5), but is it credible that armies from Agade in the north of the Mesopotamian plain could have been transported to the Oman peninsula to wage a successful campaign? It seems very hard to believe. Nor is silver found on the Oman peninsula. We are again left with a degree of uncertainty about the location of Magan. It has been suggested that the term was used for the area of south-west Iran bordering on the Gulf which, logistically, is more realistic. The area also has supplies of the dense black stones favoured by the Agade kings for their statues. If this identification is accepted the problem is that in the Ur III period, *c.* 2100 BC, the term Magan is certainly applied to the Oman peninsula. The ancient scribes seem to have had a rather elastic and foggy concept of location, unless Magan is another of the geographical terms which have moved from one area to another!

During the hundred years or so at the end of the third millennium, during which the Ur III kingdom was in power in Mesopotamia, the volume of trade with copper-producing Magan (Oman) builds up and Edens has suggested that by this time copper had become an essential commodity rather than a luxury, a change he first identifies in the Agade period (Edens 1992: 126). During this time settlement on Bahrain continues to expand and the occurrence of goods from the Indus valley and Iran, in addition to those from Mesopotamia, gives weight to the suggestion that its influence over the trade up and down the Gulf was expanding rapidly. By 2000 BC the process was complete and Mesopotamia's trade seems to have been entirely concentrated on Dilmun. Not only that, but it is clear that Dilmun is now centred in Bahrain. All mention of Magan disappears from the texts and most of the tower houses in Oman fall into disrepair. Copper continued to be mined, and softstone bowls are still produced, but a radical change in settlement pattern can be seen and direct foreign contact seems to be with the Indus valley and south-west Iran. International contacts still continue in the Wadi Suq period of the early second millennium and elaborate tombs were still built, so that it would be misleading to talk of collapse, but a fundamental change in the structure of the local economy can certainly be identified. There is little evidence of how the copper was conveyed from the mines to the middlemen in Dilmun, but a limited amount of typical Dilmun or Barbar pottery has been found at coastal sites such as Abraq, and on the Indian Ocean coast of the Oman peninsula, so perhaps boats from Dilmun dealt direct with the local copper merchants. A limited amount of Wadi Suq pottery has also been found on Bahrain. Nor do we know how the Mesopotamian boats were diverted from going direct to Magan. It may have been easier and cheaper for them to end their journeys on Bahrain and to buy supplies there, and perhaps the fragmented political situation in southern Mesopotamia in the post-Ur III period made it difficult to maintain such long-distance contacts.

The first 300 years of the second millennium marked the height of Dilmun's prosperity. Failaka was settled, presumably to make the transfer of goods to the cities of southern Mesopotamia easier and quicker, and although settlement of this period is poorly represented in the Eastern Province, the large numbers of grave mounds bear witness to the prosperity of this area too and to its incorporation as an integral part of Dilmun. Oddly, the archaeological evidence for contacts between Mesopotamia and Dilmun is very slight. Little pottery from Mesopotamia has been found and the often quoted iconographic parallels drawn from the stamp seals are of a rather generic sort, many equally at home in Syria. Recently, bitumen from Hit has been identified at the Qalaʿat, (Lombard pers. comm.) but other direct evidence for exports to Dilmun is hard to find. It has frequently been suggested in the past that this is because grain and other perishable goods formed the bulk of these exports. The importance of the grain trade has been overemphasized, but oils, textiles and other perishable commodities were almost certainly important. There is no evidence for native oil plants at all in the Dilmun period (Potts 1994). Equally, the only Dilmun artefacts found in Mesopotamia are a few

Dilmun seals. (Raw copper is hard to find in the archaeological record and harder still to source, while building timbers seldom survive at all.)

Copper remained the staple commodity traded until the network largely ceased to function around 1700 BC. A strong case has been put forward recently by T. Potts (1994) among others, for much of the tin used in the manufacture of Mesopotamian bronzes travelling up the Gulf as well, rather than across southern Iran, where bronzes are notably absent for much of this time. There is no doubt that the Dilmun trade was of major strategic importance to southern Mesopotamia in the first quarter of the second millennium. The foreign connections of Dilmun extended far beyond Mesopotamia, however, to north Syria, to Anatolia, to Eastern Iran, the Indus valley and even to Central Asia. Goods from all these regions can be identified, although much more work needs to be done on clarifying the mechanics by which they arrived. The goods were valuable and varied, lapis lazuli, beads, quality timbers and, if the texts are to be believed, peacocks and other exotic animals.

THE DECLINE OF DILMUN

Sometime in the eighteenth century the prosperity of Dilmun began to decline (Crawford 1996). There is evidence at the Qala'at for a break in the sequence of occupation levels at this time, though this is not now regarded as the dramatic hiatus which was sometimes proposed. Slightly later the Barbar temple was also abandoned. At Saar some of the houses went out of use, central control of the planning of the settlement weakened, leading to shacks being built out over the main road and a rabbit-warren of small rooms being built in the north-west of the town. However, at least one substantial villa, House 53, remained in use and the temple, too, apparently survived for an unknown length of time indicating some residual prosperity. Settlement also continues on the island of Failaka, although the pottery corpus shows an increase in the amount of Mesopotamian related shapes (Højlund 1989a). Current work on the burial mounds at al Hajjar, al Maqsha and Hamad Town also suggests that a gradual change can be identified. Some continuity now can be seen between the grave goods and the burial rites of the late Early Dilmun and the succeeding Kassite periods (Denton 1994). The old idea of a dramatic collapse at the heart of Dilmun needs to be revised, but the evidence for a marked economic decline demonstrated by the eventual abandonment of sites like Barbar, Saar and Diraz, is overwhelming.

The reasons for this decline lie outside Dilmun itself and relate to the complex international politics of the period in both Mesopotamia and the Indus valley. The events which led to the end of the mature Harappan cities in the Indus valley are still a matter for discussion; recent work suggests that Harappa itself was in decline as early as 1900 although a less urbanized late Harappan culture survived further south until as late as 1500 BC (Kenoyer 1991). It is clear that the economic consequences of this recession were felt far beyond the Indus itself. The trade routes linking Central Asia with Harappan ports like Lothal seem to have fallen into disuse and, probably as a result of this, the long distance trade up the Gulf and into Mesopotamia also ceases because the precious raw materials like lapis lazuli, and perhaps tin, which had formed an important element in the trade were no longer available for export. The native luxuries were no longer being manufactured either (Chakrabati 1995: 139) and in the straitened economic circumstances prevailing in the Indus valley there was, presumably, little demand for foreign imports from Mesopotamia or the Gulf.

The Mesopotamian evidence

An even more severe blow to the economy of Dilmun seems to have been struck by the activities of Hammurabi of Babylon. By *c.* 1800 BC the area south and east of modern Baghdad was a mosaic of small warring states of which Babylon was to become the most important. Shamshi-Adad, the ruler of Assyria to the north, seems to have exercised a measure of restraint on lesser kings, but after his death and the gradual disintegration of the old Assyrian Empire under his two sons, Hammurabi began to assimilate areas previously under their control into the kingdom of Babylon. Having consolidated his hold on the Sumerian plain by his defeats of Isin and Uruk early in his reign, he was able to take advantage of the relative weakness of Assyria to move first against Eshnunna east of the Tigris, and then against Larsa, the last important independent kingdom in the south, in his thirtieth year. His defeat of Larsa also gave him control of Ur, previously the main port of entry for goods from the Gulf. The city was already in economic decline and he was content to let it stagnate, perhaps because he already had his sights set on another prize. In his thirty-third and thirty-fifth years Hammurabi moved decisively against Mari on the middle Euphrates. Not only was Mari a rich prize in itself with its magnificent palaces, but it was the key to the control of the central Euphrates and to the rich traffic in imports from Anatolia and the Mediterranean. Mari's territory apparently extended as far as the confluence of the Balikh and Euphrates rivers and included the great canal running east of the Euphrates which was built especially to facilitate the flow of goods within its territory. Once Mari was in his hands Hammurabi could hope to benefit from the tolls levied on these goods and even more significantly, to ensure a reliable supply of basic raw materials such as copper and timber from Anatolia. Ur had become redundant and Dilmun had ceased to have a monopoly over these commodities.

Babylon's control of the middle Euphrates, which facilitated contacts as far north as Emar and Karkemish, meant that copper could now be easily acquired from Anatolia, by water, tax free, through friendly territory. In addition, copper was beginning to trickle into Mesopotamia from the mines on Cyprus, travelling east from the Mediterranean coast to the nearest point on the Euphrates from where it could be easily shipped downstream to Babylonia. As Leemans suggested (Leemans 1960: 93) this was a source whose importance was to increase greatly in the years which followed. The earliest references to Cyprus copper come from Mari in the Old Babylonian period and a text dated to the fifth year of Samsu-iluna, Hammurabi's successor, talks of copper from both Cyprus and Dilmun, another indication that some trade continued with this area in the early Old Babylonian period (Millard 1973: 212). In addition, access to the much sought-after timbers of Lebanon, used for prestige buildings since the middle of the third millennium, was also improved by control of the river route, while less exotic timbers were easily obtainable from central Anatolia.

Other materials travelled by this route. The haematite favoured for the first time by seal-cutters in the Old Babylonian period also came from Anatolia (Moorey 1994). Chlorite, which was the most common material used for the manufacture of seals in the Ur III period, and which is freely available in the Oman peninsula, almost disappears from the seal-makers' repertoire in the Old Babylonian period (Sax *et al.* 1993).

The difficulty for the Dilmun traders of competing with Anatolian raw materials must have been further enhanced by what can be described as the scorched earth policy of Hammurabi and his successor Samsu-Iluna against the great southern cities of the Sumerian plain. We saw above that the decline of Ur, one of the most important of them, (Gasche 1989) had apparently begun even earlier under Larsa rule. Hammurabi seems to have had no interest in rehabilitating it, but in Samsu-Iluna's eighth year Larsa led a successful revolt against Babylon and Ur seems to have become something of a political football. Control passed rapidly between the two kingdoms with Samsu-Iluna recapturing it briefly in his tenth year when he destroyed its walls. Some small-scale resettlement took place after this, but this destruction seems to have been the final blow and prosperity did not return until around 1400 BC (van de Mieroop 1992). The picture at Ur is not unique, but seems to have been repeated across much of the southern plain as the irrigation system collapsed and people were forced to move from the area. Even the old religious capital of Nippur seems to have been abandoned after Samsu-Iluna's thirtieth year (Stone 1987: 26–7). With such widespread economic and political disruption it is difficult to see what market there would have been for imports from the Gulf even if an alternative port of entry had been found. This abandonment of the south seems to have lasted as long as 200 years until the advent of the Kassite kings, although the marshes became the centre of the so-called Sealand dynasty of which almost nothing is known. Even the Sealand capital has not been identified and few items of its material culture can be confidently identified. All that remain are a few textual references.

The evidence from Elam

One other country is known to have been involved in economic transactions with Dilmun at the height of its prosperity and that is Elam in south-west Iran. Unfortunately the history of this region in the early second millennium is not well known, but Susa seems to have enjoyed a period of expansion and prosperity in the Old Babylonian period under the rule of the so-called Sukkalmahs or Great Regents. Contacts with Dilmun certainly still existed. A tablet dated to the reign of Kutir-Nahhunte 1, *c*. 1730–1700 BC, lists the delivery of 17.5 minas of silver to Susa by Dilmunites (Leemans 1960: 217), though it is not known if this represents trade goods, tribute, taxes or a gift, and a temple to Inzac of Dilmun stood in the city at this time. In addition, a number of Dilmun seals have been found there and Dilmun motifs can be identified in the local glyptic repertoire (al-Gailani Werr 1986). The evidence suggests that it was trade with a resurgent Susa which helped to succour the last years of Dilmun, although no trace of Elamite influence can be seen on Failaka, the closest part of Dilmun.

The slow decline of Dilmun was the result of a complex interplay of political and economic factors in other parts of the ancient world. Both the northern and southern ends of the Gulf trade route suffered major economic problems at the same time as the result of political upheavals in the north and possible environmental degradation in the Indus valley. One result of this was that the middlemen in Dilmun and the producers in Magan found their livelihood cut from under their feet. It is this combination of circumstances which can be seen as the cause of the decline in the importance and prosperity of Dilmun from the eighteenth century onwards. The decline in prosperity in Magan, as we have already seen, began rather earlier when Dilmun gained sole control of the Mesopotamian trade. The loss of this overseas trade meant a dramatic contraction in Dilmun's economic prosperity, but the region continued to develop along its own path and was to appear again on the world stage in a different role with the arrival of the Kassites in the second half of the second millennium.

The crucial importance of international trade in the development of the cultures of the Gulf has led to a tendency in the past for scholars to see them in terms of their relations with the old 'High Civilizations' of Mesopotamia, Iran and the Indus valley. This is to distort the history of a region which saw the emergence of indigenous cultures uniquely well adapted to the harsh conditions on the Arabian peninsula, in touch with the outside world but with a character which was distinctively their own. It is possible to distinguish two main threads in this development, that linking the lands of the northern Gulf and that which can be seen on the Oman peninsula. The former reaches its most distinctive form in the early second millennium when Dilmun was at its most powerful, while the second can be seen in the Umm-an-Nar and Wadi Suq cultures. The rediscovery of these cultures has been one of the most important events of recent years for the history of the ancient Near East.

BIBLIOGRAPHY

Adams, R.McC. 1977. Saudi Arabian archaeological reconnaissance. *Atlal* I. 21–40.

Aitken, M.J. 1990. *Science-based dating in archaeology*. Longman. London.

Akkermans, P. 1993. *Villages in the steppe: late Neolithic settlement and subsistence in the Balikh, North Syria*. Michigan: Ann Arbor.

al-Gailani Werr, L. 1986. Gulf (Dilmun) style cylinder seals. *PSAS* 16: 199–201.

al Khalifa, Shaikha Haya Ali and Michael Rice ed. 1986. *Bahrain through the Ages*. Kegan Paul International.

al Mughannam, Ali S. *et al.* 1986. Excavations of the Dhahran burial mounds. 3rd season 1405/1985–'86. *Atlal* 10: 9–28.

al Nashef, Khalid 1986. The deities of Dilmun. In *BTAA*: 340–66.

al Sindi, Khalid 1994. *Catalogue of seals in the Bahrain National Museum* I (Arabic).

al-Tikriti, Abdul Kader 1975. Diraz excavation and its chronological position. *Dilmun* 8: 16–20.

al Tikriti, W.Y. 1981. *A reconsideration of the late 4th and early 3rd millennium BC in the Arabian Gulf with special reference to the UAE*. Unpublished Ph.D thesis. Cambridge.

 1985. Archaeological investigations on Ghanadha island 1982–1984: Further evidence for the coastal Umm an-Nar culture. *AUAE* IV: 9–19.

 1989a. The excavations at Bidya, Fujairah: the 3rd and 2nd millennia BC culture. *AUAE* V: 101–11.

 1989b. Umm-an-Nar culture in the Northern Emirates: third millennium BC tombs at Ajman. *AUAE* V: 89–100.

Algaze, Guillermo 1993. *The Uruk world picture*. Chicago.

Allchin, Bridget and Raymond 1982. *The rise of civilization in India and Pakistan*. Cambridge.

Alster, B. 1983. Dilmun, Bahrain and the alleged Paradise in Sumerian myth and literature. In Dilmun: New studies in the archaeology and early history of Bahrain. *BBVO* 2: 39–74.

Amiet, P. 1986. *L'âge des échanges inter-iraniens 3500–1700 avant J-C*. Paris.

Andersen, H. Hellmuth 1986. The Barbar temple: stratigraphy, architecture and interpretation. In *BTAA*: 165–77.

Arabian Gulf Intelligence. Reprint 1985. *Selections from the records of the Bombay Government New Series, no. XXIV, 1856*. Edited and compiled by R. Hughes Thomas. Oleander Press.

Aurenche, O. 1987. *Chronologies du Proche Orient*. BAR International series 379. Oxford.

Barger, Thomas G. 1969. A seal found in Arabia. *Archaeology* 22: 140.

Benton, J.D. 1996. *Excavations at Al Sufouh: a third millennium site in the Emirate of Dubai. Abiel* I. Brepols.

Bibby, G. 1972. *Looking for Dilmun*. Penguin.

 1973. *Preliminary survey in East Arabia 1968. JASP* 12.

 1986. The origins of the Dilmun civilization. In *BTAA*: 108–15.

Boucharlat, R. *et al.* 1991. Note on an Ubaid-pottery site in the Emirate of Umm al-Qaiwain. *AAE* 2: 65–71.

Bowersock, G.W. 1986. Tylos and Tyre: Bahrain in the Graeco-Roman world. In *BTAA* 399–40.

Brunswick, R.H. Jr 1989. Culture, history, environment and economy, as seen from an Umm an-Nar settlement: evidence from test excavations at Bat, Oman. *JOS* 10: 9–50.

Brunswig, R.H. *et al.* 1983. New Indus type and related seals from the Near East. *BBVO* 2 101–15.

Burrows, E. 1928. *Tilmun, Bahrain, Paradise*. Scriptura sacra et monumenta orientis antiqui.

Calvet, Yves 1984. La fouille de l'âge du Bronze (G3). In Failaka fouilles françaises. 1983. *Travaux de la Maison de l'Orient* 9. Lyon.

Calvet, Y. and J. Gachet 1990. Failaka fouilles françaises. 1986–1988. *Travaux de la Maison de l'Orient* 18. Lyon.

Calvet,Y and J-F. Salles. 1986. Failaka fouilles françaises.1984–1985. *Travaux de la Maison de l'Orient* 12. Lyon.

Cardi, B. de 1982. Excavations at Tawi Silaim and Tawi Sa'id in the Sharqiya 1978. *JOS* 5: 61–94.

 1986. Some aspects of Neolithic settlement in Bahrain and adjacent regions. In *BTAA* 87–93.

 1988. The grave goods from Shimal Tomb 6 in Ras al Khaimah, UAE. In *Araby the blest*. Potts ed. Copenhagen: 45–72.

 1989. Harappan finds from Tomb 6 at Shimal, Ras al Khaimah, UAE. In *South Asian Archaeology 1985*. ed. Frifelt, K. and P. Sørensen: 9–14.

Card, B. de ed. 1978. *Qatar Archaeological Report. Excavations 1973*. Oxford.

Cardi, B. de *et al.* 1976. Excavations and survey in Oman 1974–1975. *JOS* 2: 101–88.

 1979. Excavations at Tawi Silaim and Tawi Sa'id. *JOS* 5: 61–94.

Carter, R. 1997. The Wadi Suq period in S.E. Arabia: a reappraisal. *PSAS*.

Chakrabati, D.K. 1990. *The external trade of the Indus civilization*. Delhi.

 1995. *The archaeology of ancient Indian cities*. Oxford.

Childe, V.G. 1950. The urban revolution. In *Town Planning Review* 21. i: 3–17.

Ciarli, R. 1990. Fragments of stone vessels. Two case studies Failaka and Shahr-i-Sokhta. In *South Asian Archaeology 1987*. ed. Taddei, Maurizio. Rome: 475–49.

Cleuziou, Serge 1981. Oman peninsula in the early second millennium. In Hartel, ed. *South Asian Archaeology 1979*.

 1989. Excavations at Hili 8: a preliminary report on the 4th–7th campaigns. *Archaeology in the United Arab Emirates* V: 61–87.

 1994. Black boats of Magan. In *South Asian Archaeology. Helsinki 1993*. ed. Koskenniemi S. and Parpola A. Helsinki: 745–61.

Cleuziou, S. *et al.* 1981. *Fouilles à Umm Jidr (Bahrain)*. Paris.

 1994. Cachets inscrits de la fin du IIIe millénaire av. notre ère à Ras al-Junayz, Sultanat d'Oman. *Académie des Inscriptions et Belles-Lettres Paris*. Avril-Juin: 453–68.

Cleuziou, S. and L. Constantini 1980. Premiers éléments sur l'agriculture protohistoire de l'Arabie orientale. *Paléorient* 6: 255–61.

Cleuziou, S. and M. Tosi 1989. The southeastern frontier of the ancient near East. In *South Asian Archaeology 1985*. ed. Frifelt, K. and P. Sørensen:15–48.

Cleuziou, S. and B. Vogt 1985. Tomb A at Hili North. In *South Asian Archaeology 1983*. 7i. ed. J. Schotsmans and M. Taddei. Naples: 249–78.

Conan, Jacques and Odile Deschesne. 1996. *Le Bitumene à Suse*. Musée du Louvre/Elf.

Coppa, A. *et al.* 1985. The Prehistoric graveyard of Ra's al-Hamra (RH5). *JOS* 8: 97–108.

Cornwall, P.B. 1946. On the location of Dilmun. *BASOR* 103, 3–11.

Costa, P.M. and M. Tosi ed. 1989. *Oman studies: papers on the archaeology and history of Oman*. Rome.

Costa, P.M and T.J. Wilkinson 1987. Settlement and copper exploitation in the 'Arja area. *JOS* 9.

Crawford, Harriet. 1991a. *Sumer and the Sumerians*. Cambridge.

 1991b. Seals from the first season's excavations at Saar, Bahrain. *Cambridge Archaeological Journal* 1: 255–62.

 1993. London–Bahrain Archaeological Expedition: excavations at Saar 1991. *AAE* 4: 1–19.

 1996. The decline of Dilmun. *PSAS* 26: 13–22.

Crawford, Harriet and Khalid al-Sindi 1995. A seal in the collections of the National Museum, Bahrain. *AAE* 6: 1–4.

1996. A 'Hut pot' in the National Museum Bahrain. *AAE* 7: 140–2.

Crawford, Harriet, Robert Killick and Jane Moon, ed. 1997. *The Dilmun temple at Saar*. London.

Cribb, Roger 1991. *Nomads in archaeology*. Cambridge.

Delongeville, R. and P. Sanlaville 1987. Evidence from dates, geomorphology and archaeology. In *Chronologies du Proche Orient* ed. O. Aurenche. BAR International series 379. ii.

Delougaz, Pinhas 1952. *Pottery from the Diyala region*. Chicago.

Denton, Branwen E. 1994. Pottery, cylinder seals, and stone vessels from the cemeteries of al-Hajjar, al-Maqsha and Hamad Town on Bahrain. *JAAE* 5: 121–51.

Dobney, K.M. and D. Jaques. 1994. Animal bones from Saar. *JAAE* 5: 106–20.

Doe, Brian 1986. The Barbar temple: the masonry. In *BTAA* 186–91.

During-Caspers, Elizabeth C.L. 1980. *The Bahrain Tumuli*. Belgium.

1986. Animal designs and Gulf chronology. In *BTAA*: 286–304.

1991. A Harappan bronze found in the Jefferson tumulus on Bahrain. In *Golf-Archäologie, Buch am Erlbach*: Schippmann *et al.* ed. 159–74.

Edens, Christopher 1992. Dynamics of trade in the ancient Mesopotamian 'World System'. *American Anthropology* 94: 118–39.

1994. On the Complexity of complex societies: Structure, Power and Legitimation in Kassite Babylonia. In *Chiefdoms and early States in the Near East*. ed. Stein, Gil and M. Rothman. Prehistory Press.

Englund, Robert 1983. Dilmun in the archaic Uruk corpus. In Dilmun: New studies in the archaeology and early history of Bahrain. *BBVO* 2.

Finley, M.I. 1954. Reprinted 1971. *The world of Odysseus*. Penguin.

Flavin, K. and E. Shepherd 1994. Fishing in the Gulf: preliminary investigations at an Ubaid site, Dalma (UAE). *PSAS* 24: 115–34.

Frifelt, Karen. 1975a. A possible link between the Jemdet Nasr and the Umm an-Nar graves of Oman. *JOS* 1: 56–80.

1975b. On prehistoric settlement and chronology of the Oman peninsula. Plan of Hili 1. *East and West* 25: 359–424.

1976. Evidence of a third millennium town in Oman. *JOS* 2: 57–74.

1980. 'Jemdet Nasr' graves on the Oman peninsula. In Death in Mesopotamia. ed. B. Alster. Mesopotamia 8. Copenhagen.

1986. Burial mounds near Ali excavated by the Danish expedition. In *BTAA*: 125–34.

1991. The island of Umm an-Nar. Third millennium graves. *JASP* XXVI. i.

1995. The island of Umm an-Nar. The third millennium settlement. *JASP* XXVI. ii.

Frohlich, Bruno and Ali Mughannum 1985. Excavations of the Dhahran burial mounds. *Atlal* 9.I: 9–40.

Gadd, C.J. 1932. Reprinted 1979. Seals of ancient Indian style found at Ur. *Proceedings of the British Academy* 18: 3–22.

Gale, Rowena 1994. Charcoal from an Early Dilmun settlement at Saar, Bahrain. *AAE* 5: 229–35.

Gasche, H. 1989. La Babylonie au 17ème siècle avant notre ère: approche archéologique, problemes et perspectives. *Mesopotamian History and Environment Memoirs* II. Ghent.

Gelb, I.J. 1970. Makkan and Meluhha in Early Mesopotamian sources. *Révue d'Assyriologie* 64: 1–8.

Gentelle, P. and K. Frifelt 1989. About the distribution of 3rd millennium graves in the Ibri region of Oman. In *Oman Studies*. ed. Costa, P.M. and Tosi M.: 119–26.

Glassner, J.J. 1989. Mesopotamian textual evidence on Magan/Makan in the late 3rd millennium texts. In *Oman Studies* ed. Costa, P.M. and Tosi, M.: 181–92.

Glob, P.V. 1968. *Al Bahrain*. Denmark.

Glover, Emily 1995. Molluscan evidence for diet and environment at Saar in the early second mil-
     lennium BC. *AAE* 6: 157–79.
Golding, M. 1974. Evidence for pre-Seleucid occupation of Eastern Arabia. *PSAS* 4: 19–32.
Groneberg, Brigitte 1992. Le Golfe Arabo-Persique vu depuis Mari. In *Florilegium marianum.*
     Receuil d'études en l'honneur de Michel Fleury. Paris: 69–79.
Haerinck, E. 1994. More prehistoric finds from the United Arab Emirates. *AAE* 5: 153–57.
Hanson, S. 1992. *'Isin-Larsa' period incised and white filled Grey Ware.* Unpublished BA thesis.
     Institute of Archaeology, UCL.
Harper, Prudence *et al.* 1992. *The Royal City of Susa.* Metropolitan Museum of Art.
Hartel, H. ed. 1981. *South Asian Archaeology 1979.* Berlin.
Häser, J. 1990. Softstone vessels of the second millennium BC in the Gulf region. *PSAS* 20: 43–54.
Hastings *et al.* 1975. Oman in the third millennium BCE. *JOS* I: 9–56.
Hauptmann, A. *et al.* 1988. Early copper metallurgy in Oman. In *The beginning of the use of metals*
     and alloys. ed. Robert Maddin. MIT: 34–51.
Heimpel, W. 1987. Das Untere Meer. *Zeitschrift für Assyriologie* 77: 29–91.
Heinz, Marlies 1994. Die Keramik aus Saar, Bahrain. *Baghdader Mitteilungen* 25: 119–307.
Hill, H. and P. Jacobsen 1990. *Old Babylonian Public Buildings in the Diyala region.* Chicago.
Hillier, Bill and Alan Penn 1991. Visible colleges: structure and randomness in the place of discov-
     ery. *Science in Context* 4: 23–49.
Hoch, E. 1979. Reflections on prehistoric life at Umm an-Nar (Trucial Oman) based on faunal remains
     from the third millennium B.C. In Taddei, M ed. *South Asian Archaeology 1977*: 589–638.
Højlund, Flemming 1987. Failaka/Dilmun. The second millennium settlement. The Bronze Age
     pottery. *JASP* XVII. ii.
     1989a. The formation of the Dilmun state and the Amorite tribes. *PSAS* 19: 46–57.
     1989b. Dilmun and the Sealand. *North Akkad Project Reports* 2: 9–19.
Højlund, Flemming and H. Hellmuth Andersen 1994. Qalaʿat al-Bahrain I. The northern city wall
     and the Islamic fortress. *JASP* XXX.i
Howard-Carter, T. 1972. Johns Hopkins University reconnaissance expedition to the Arab-Iranian
     Gulf. *BASOR* 207.
Howard-Carter, T. 1987. Dilmun: at sea or not at sea? *J. Cuneiform Studies* 39: 54–117.
Humphries, J.H. 1974. Harvard archaeological survey in Oman: II – some later prehistoric sites in
     the Sultanate of Oman. *PSAS* 4: 49–76.
Huot, J-L. 1989. 'Ubaidian village of Lower Mesopotamia. Permanence and evolution from 'Ubaid
     0 to 'Ubaid 4 as seen from tell el'Oueili. In *Upon this foundation.* ed. Henrickson. E. and I.
     Theusen. Copenhagen.
Ibrahim, Moawiyah 1982. *Excavations of the Arab Expedition at Sâr el-Jisr. Bahrain.* Ministry of
     Information, Bahrain.
Inizan, M-L. 1980. Site à poterie obeidienne à Qatar. In *L'archéologie de l'Iraq.* ed. Barrelet. M-T.
     CNRS. Paris.
Inizan, M-L. ed. 1988. *Préhistoire à Qatar, mission archéologique à Qatar 2.* Paris.
Kapel, H. 1967. Atlas of the Stone-Age cultures of Qatar. Reports of the Danish Archaeological
     Expedition to the Gulf I. *JASP* 6.
Kennet, D. and D. Connolly 1995. *The towers of Ras al-Khaimah.* Tempus Reparatum. Oxford.
Kenoyer, Jonathan Mark 1991. Urban process in the Indus tradition: a preliminary model from
     Harappa. In Harappa excavations 1986–1990 ed. Richard H. Meadow. *Monographs in World*
     Archaeology 3. Wisconsin: 29–60.
Kent, Susan ed. 1990. *Domestic architecture and the use of space.* Cambridge.
Kervran, Monique ed. 1988. *Bahrain in the 16th century: an impregnable island.* Ministry of
     Information. Bahrain.

Killick, R.G. *et al.* 1991. London–Bahrain Archaeological Expedition: 1990 excavations at Saar, Bahrain. *AAE* 2. 2: 107–37.

Killick, Robert *et al.* 1997. London–Bahrain Archaeological Expedition: 1994 and 1995 excavations at Saar, Bahrain. *AAE* 8: 86–98.

Kjaerum, Poul 1980. Seals of 'Dilmun type' from Failaka, Kuwait. *PSAS* 10: 45–54.

   1983. Failaka/Dilmun. The second millennium settlement. I.i. The stamp and cylinder seals. *JASP* XVII. i.

   1994. Stamp seals. In *Qala'at al Bahrain I*. ed. Højlund, F.

Kohl, P.L. 1974. *Seeds of upheaval: the production of chlorite at Tepe Yahya and an analysis of commodity production and trade in Southwest Asia in the third millennium*. Harvard Ph.D dissertation, Ann Arbor.

   1984. *Central Asia. Palaeolithic beginnings to the Iron Age*. Paris.

Kohl, P., G. Harbottle and E.V. Sayre. 1979. Physical and chemical analysis of soft stone vessels from Southwest Asia. *Archaeometry* 21: 131–59.

Konishi, M.A. 1994. *Ain Umm es-Sujur. An interim report 1993/4*. Tokyo.

Kramer, S.N. 1963. Dilmun: quest for Paradise. *Antiquity* 37: 111–15.

Lamberg-Karlovsky, C.C. 1970. *Excavations at Tepe Yahya Iran. 1967–1969. Progress report 1*. Cambridge, Mass.

   1986. Death in Dilmun. In *BTAA* 157–64.

Larsen, C.E. 1983a. The early environment and hydrology of ancient Bahrain. *BBVO* 2: 3–34.

   1983b. *Life and land use on the Bahrain islands*. University of Chicago Press.

Leemans, W.F. 1960. *Foreign trade in the Old Babylonian period*. Leiden.

Lombard, P. 1988. The Salt Mine site and the 'Hasaean period' of Northeastern Arabia. In *Araby the blest*: Potts, D.T ed. 117–36.

Lombard, P. and M. Kervran. ed. 1989. *Bahrain National Museum. Archaeological Collections* I. Ministry of Information, Bahrain.

Lorimer, John G. reprinted 1970. *Gazeteer of the Persian Gulf, Oman and Central Arabia*. 6 vols. Farnborough. Hants. Holland Printers.

Lowe, A. 1986. Bronze age burial mounds on Bahrain. *Iraq* XLVIII: 73–84.

Mallowan, M.E.L. and J. Cruikshank Rose 1935. Excavations at Tell Arpachiyah 1933. *Iraq* II. i: 1–178.

Marshall, Sir John 1931. *Mohenjo-daro and the Indus civilization*. 3 vols. London.

Masry, Abdullah Hassan 1974. *Prehistory in Northeastern Arabia: the problem of interregional interaction*. Field Research Projects. Coconut Grove. Florida.

   1978. A reply to J. Oates *et al.*, 'Seafaring merchants of Ur?'. *Antiquity* LII. 204: 46–7.

Mclure, H.A. and N.Y. al Shaikh 1993. Palaeogeography of an Ubaid archaeological site, Saudi Arabia. *AAE* 4. 2: 107–25.

Méry, S. 1991. Origine et production des récipients de terre cuite dans la peninsula d'Oman à l'âge du Bronze. *Paléorient* 17: 51–78.

Millard, A.R. 1973. Cypriot copper in Babylonia. *Journal of Cuneiform Studies* 25: 211–13.

Ministry of Information. nd. *Guide to the Barbar temple*. Bahrain.

Miroschedi, P. de 1973. Vases et objets en stéatite susiens du musée du Louvre. *DAFI* 3: 9–79.

Mitchell, T.C. 1986. Indus and Gulf type seals from Ur. *BTAA*: 278–85.

Moon, Jane *et al.* 1995. London–Bahrain Archaeological Expedition excavations at Saar: 1993 season. *AAE* 6: 139–56.

Moon, Jane and Robert Killick 1995. A Dilmun residence. In *Beitrage zur Kulturgeschichte Vorderasiens. Festschrift für Rainer Michael Boehmer*. ed. Finkbeiner, U. *et al.* Von Zabern, Mainz.

Moorey, P.R.S. 1985. *Materials and manufacture in ancient Mesopotamia*. BAR International series 287. Oxford.

1994. *Ancient Mesopotamian materials and industries*. Oxford.

Morris, Ian 1992. *Death-ritual and social structure in classical antiquity*. Cambridge.

Mortensen, Peder 1970. On the dating of the Barbar Temple. *Kuml*: 385–98.

1986. The Barbar temple: its chronology and foreign relations reconsidered. In *BTAA*: 178–85.

Mughal, Rafique 1983. *The Dilmun burial complex at Sar: the 1980–1982 excavations*. Ministry of Information. Bahrain.

Mynors, S. 1983. An examination of Mesopotamian ceramics using petrographic and neutron activation analysis. *Proceedings of the 22nd symposium of Archaeometry*. Bradford: 277–87.

Naval Intelligence. 1944. Geographical Handbook. *Iraq and the Persian Gulf*. London.

Nayeem, M.A. 1990. *Saudi Arabia*. Hyderabad publishers.

1992. *Bahrain*. Hyderabad publishers.

Nesbitt, Mark 1993. Archaeobotanical evidence for early Dilmun diet at Saar, Bahrain. *JAAE* 4:20–47.

Nissen, H.J. 1993. The context of the emergence of writing in Mesopotamia and Iran. In *Early Mesopotamia and Iran*. ed. Curtis, John. British Museum Press.

Oates, Joan 1960. Ur and Eridu, the Prehistory. *Iraq* XXII: 32–50.

1978. Ubaid Mesopotamia and its relation to the Gulf countries. In de Cardi ed. *Qatar Archaeological Report. Excavation 1973*. Oxford.

1984. Ubaid Mesopotamia reconsidered. In The Hilly flanks: essays presented to Robert J. Braidwood. Oriental Institute Chicago. *SOAC* 36.

1986. The Gulf in Prehistory. In *BTAA* 79–86.

Oates, J. *et al.* 1977. Seafaring merchants of Ur? *Antiquity* 51. 221–34.

Orchard, J. 1995. The origins of agricultural settlement in the al-Hajar region. In *Iraq* LVII: 145–58.

Orchard, J. and G. Stranger 1994. Third millennium oasis towns and environmental constraints in the al-Hajar region. *Iraq* LVI: 63–100.

Oppenheim, A.L. 1954. The seafaring merchants of Ur. *JAOS* 74. 6–17.

Palgrave, W.G. 1883. *Personal narrative of a year's journey through Central and Eastern Arabia. (1862–63)* London.

Pettinato, Giovanni 1983. Dilmun nella documentazione di Ebla. *BBVO* 2.

1991. *Ebla*. Baltimore and London.

Pézard, M. 1914. Mission à Bender-Bouchir. *Publications de la Mission Archéologique de Perse* 15.

Piesinger, C.M. 1983. *The Legacy of Dilmun*. Unpublished Ph.D dissertation, University of Wisconsin–Madison.

Possehl, G. 1979. *Ancient Cities of the Indus*. Faridabad. India.

Pottier, M-H. 1984. *Matérial funéraire de la Bactriane méridionale de l'age du bronze*. Paris.

Potts, D.T. 1981. Towards an integrated history of culture change in the Arabian Gulf area: notes on Dilmun, Magan and the economy of ancient Sumer. *JOS* 4: 29–51.

1986a. Eastern Arabia and the Oman peninsula during the late 4th and early 3rd millennia BC. In *Gamdat Nasr: period or regional style?* ed. U. Finkbeiner: 121–70. Weisbaden.

1986b Dilmun's further relations; the Syro-Anatolian evidence from the third and second millennia. In *BTAA*: 389–98.

1989. *Miscellanea Hasaitica*. CNI publications 9. Copenhagen.

1990a. *The Arabian Gulf in Antiquity*. vol. I. *From prehistory to the fall of the Achaemenid empire*. Clarendon Press, Oxford.

1990b. *A prehistoric mound in the Emirate of Umm al-Qaiwain*. Munksgaard.

1993a. The late prehistoric, protohistoric and early historic periods in Eastern Arabia (*c.* 5,000–1200 BC). *Journal of World Prehistory* 7.2: 163–212.

1993b. Four seasons of excavation at Tell Abraq (1989–1993*) Journal of PSAS* 23: 117–26.

1993c. A new Bactrian find from southeastern Asia. *Antiquity* 67. 256: 591–95.

1993d. Rethinking some aspects of trade in the Arabian Gulf. *World Archaeology* 24.3: 423–40.

1994. Contributions to the agrarian history of E. Arabia. The cultivars. *JAAE* 5. 4: 236–75.

Potts, D.T. ed. 1983. Dilmun – new studies in the archaeology and early history of Bahrain. *BBVO* 2.

1988. *Araby the blest*. Copenhagen.

Potts, D.T. *et al*. 1978. Comprehensive Archaeological Survey programme. a) Preliminary report on the second phase of the Eastern Province survey 1397/1977. *Atlal* 2: 7–28.

Potts, T. 1994. *Mesopotamia and the east. An archaeological and historical study of foreign relations 3400–2000 BC*. Oxford University Committee for Archaeology.

Rao, S.R. 1986. Trade and cultural contacts between Bahrain and India in the third and second millennia BC. *BTAA*: 376–82.

Reade, J. and R. Burleigh 1978. The 'Ali cemetery: old excavations and radiocarbon dating. *JOS* 4: 75–83.

Renfrew, C. and J. Dixon. 1976 Obsidian in Western Asia. A review. In *Problems in economic and social archaeology*. ed. G. de G. Sieveking *et al*. London.

Renfrew, C. and P. Bahn 1991. *Archaeology: theories methods and practice*. London.

Rice, Michael 1972. The grave complex at al-Hajjar, Bahrain. *PSAS* 2.

1985. *Search for the Paradise Land*. London.

1988. Al Hajjar revisited: the grave complex at al Hajjar. *PSAS* 18: 79–94.

1994. *The Archaeology of the Arabian Gulf*. London.

Rice, Michael ed. 1984. *Dilmun discovered*. Department of Antiquities of the State of Bahrain and Longmans.

Roaf, Michael 1976. Excavations at al-Markh, Bahrain. *PSAS* 6: 144–60.

1978. *A report on the work of the British Archaeological Expedition to Bahrain. 1977/1978*. Unpublished preliminary report.

Roaf, Michael and Jane Galbraith 1994. Pottery and p-values: 'Seafaring merchants of Ur' re-examined. *Antiquity* 68. 61: 770–83.

Safar, F. M.A. Mustafa and Seton Lloyd 1981. *Eridu*. State Organisation of Antiquities. Baghdad.

Salles, J-F. 1984. Failaka fouilles françaises. 1983. *Travaux de la Maison de l'Orient* 9. Lyon.

Sax, M. *et al*. 1993. The availability of raw materials for Near Eastern cylinder seals during the Akkadian, post-Akkadian and Ur III periods. *Iraq* LV: 77–90.

Schmandt-Besserat, D. 1980. Envelopes that bear the first writing. In *Technology and Culture* 21: 357–85.

Schotsmans, J. and M. Taddei 1985. *South Asian Archaeology 1983*. 7.I. Naples.

Sollberger, E. and J-R. Kupper 1971. *Les inscriptions royales sumériennes et akkadiennes*. Paris.

Srivastava, K.M. 1991. *Madinat Hamad burial mounds 1984–85*. National Museum. Bahrain.

Stone, E. 1987. *Nippur neighbourhoods*. Chicago.

Stronach, David 1961. The excavations at Ras al 'Amiya. *Iraq* XXIII: 95–137.

Tixier, Jacques 1986. The prehistory of the Gulf: recent finds. *BTAA*: 76–8.

Tosi, M. 1975. Notes on the distribution and extraction of natural resources in ancient Oman. *JOS* 1: 187–206.

1986. Early maritime cultures of the Arabian gulf and the Indian Ocean. *BTAA*: 94–107.

Vallat, François 1983. Le dieu Enzak: une divinité Dilmunite venerée à Suse. In *BBVO* 2.

Van de Mieroop, Marc 1992. Society and enterprise in Old Babylonian Ur. *BBVO* 12.

Vine, Peter 1993. *Bahrain National Museum*. Immel. London.

Vogt, B. 1985a. *Zur Chronologie und Entwicklung der Gräber des später 4–2. Jtsd.v.Chr. auf der Halbinsel Oman*. Ph.D thesis, Göttingen.

1985b. The Umm an-Nar tomb A at Hili North: a preliminary report on three seasons of excavation 1982–1984. Archaeology in the United Arab Emirates IV: 20–38.

1994. *Asimah*. Department of Antiquities Ras al-Khaimah.

Vogt, B. and Ute Franke-Vogt ed. 1987. Shimal 1985/1986. *BBVO* 8.

Weisgerber, G. 1980. 'und Kupfer in Oman' *Der Anschnitt* 32.2/3: 62–110.

1981. Mehr als Kupfer in Oman. *Der Anschnitt* 33.5/6: 174–263.

Weisgerber, G. and H.G. Bachmann 1988. Early copper metallurgy in Oman. In *The beginning of the use of metals and alloys*. ed. Robert Maddin. MIT: 34–51.

Whitehouse, D. 1975. Sources of Carnelian in the Persian Gulf. *Antiquity* XLIX: 129–30.

Woodburn, M.A. and H.E.W. Crawford 1994. London–Bahrain Archaeological Expedition: 1991–2 excavations at Saar. *AAE* 5: 89–105.

Woolley, C.L. 1934. *Ur excavations volume II. The Royal Cemetery*. London.

Wrigley, E.A. 1969. reprinted 1973. *Population and history*. World University Library. Weidenfeld & Nicholson.

Yateem, Aisha 1992. *Bahrain memories*. Pontifex publishers. Australia.

Zaccagnini, C. 1986. The Dilmun standard and its relationship with Indus and Near Eastern weight systems. *Iraq* XLVIII: 19–23.

Zarins, J. 1978. Steatite vessels in the Riyadh museum. *Atlal* 2:65–94.

1989. Eastern Saudi Arabia and external relations: selected ceramic, steatite and textual evidence 3,500–1900BC. In *South Asian Archaeology 1985*. ed. Frifelt, K. and Per Sørensen. Curzon Press.

1990. Obsidian and the Red Sea trade. In *South Asian Archaeology 1987*. I. ed. Maurizio Taddei. Rome. 507–41.

Zarins, J. *et al*. 1979. Saudi Arabian reconnaissance 1978. *Atlal* 3: 9–38.

1984. Excavations at Dhahran south – the tumulus field (208–92). A preliminary report. *Atlal* 8: 25–54.

1992. The early settlement of south Mesopotamia. *JAOS* 112: 55–77.

Zohary, Daniel and Maria Hopf 1994. *Domestication of plants in the Old World*. 2nd ed. Oxford. Clarendon Press.

INDEX

165

DATE DUE

GAYLORD

PRINTED IN U.S.A.